FIRED:

CHALLENGING THE STATUS QUO AND SURVIVING THE AFTERMATH

Cristina Carballo-Perelman, M.D.

Table of Contents

PROLOGUE

First, let me tell you a bit about myself. This is important, because it will set the tone for the rest of this book.

I have been a subspecialty doctor for almost 30 years, including my fellowship training. During these years, I was able to work in a large medical group that brought certain specialized services to our city in the early 1970s. I went from full-time to part-time, while my daughter was growing up, to full-time again.

Seven years ago, I was given the opportunity to create and initiate an innovative, cutting-edge program to benefit our patients who suffered from a particular disease process. Thanks to this program, we were able to decrease the incidence of long term disabilities significantly.

During the growth of this program—which included funding from an outside, nonprofit organization to create a computerized data system—our private group was bought out by a larger physician group. When this happened, my immediate physician supervisor retired.

This is an important event in my story, because this physician was my "protector." In other words, he allowed me to continue to grow and manage this program. He believed in what we were doing and understood my frustration with what I believed to be the less-than-adequate care being provided by some of the other physicians. He made sure the other physicians knew about our successes, sharing all the media articles printed about us with the rest of the group, as well as the published abstracts and journal articles.

I am only telling you this so you know that I was committed to my profession, wanting to provide the very best care possible to every patient I was taking care of, to ensure that their long-term prognosis was optimized.

I also want to make sure that you, the reader, understand that my passion was giving the best care to my patients. It was never about being seen as an autocratic leader or, as I was called, a "know-it-all," a witch, or, my favorite, "ice bitch."

Yet, despite our success rate in treating our patients with expert care by MANY on our team, including other subspecialists; despite publishing a paper concerning our outcomes in a peer-reviewed journal; and despite the many accolades showered on our team and me by the community, I was fired.

Let me tell you the exact words used to do this:

"We are trying to integrate our members and build a team. You have been critical of your colleagues and therefore they refuse to send patients to the facility you work at, which impedes us building this team. Therefore, you are terminated, effective immediately." To my question, "So, you would rather fire me than put me in a room with the other physicians so we can talk about our differences in care?" there was no answer.

With those words, my career ended. Why? Because of the non-compete clause in my contract, I would have had to relocate to another state if I wanted to continue to practice. This, of course, was not happening! Had I been in my early career stage, I might have considered this, but being near the tail-end of my career, a move would have been devastating to my mental health. Challenging this dismissal as wrongful was also not possible, since again, my contract prohibited this.

And so, I felt compelled, instead, to write this book, with the hope that I would be able to help others so that they would not have to go through the same trauma I went through. Perhaps these chapters will not only help employees be able to do what is best without fear of being terminated but also help employers learn to bring grace, understanding, and compassion to their companies. Perhaps it will even inspire them to consider adopting corporate social responsibility policies—internal as well as external.

Lastly, I want to thank you for reading this. I hope it helps you in your journey through life and helps your career to flourish and, by doing so, benefits others.

DEDICATION

I dedicate this book to all those employees who have been wrongfully fired for trying to do what was best for others. Whether you were whistleblowers or simply tried to do the right thing, you paid the ultimate price. Not only did you lose monetary compensation, but you also lost faith in others.

I also dedicate this book to all the employers who were blinded by corporate greed and/or power and who now regret their actions. I hope that whatever made you regret your actions—lawsuits, bankruptcy, or otherwise—you will find a way to make amends to all those who were hurt by your actions.

Last but certainly not least, I dedicate this book to my husband, who every day reminded me that I could look at myself in the mirror and feel nothing but respect for the person looking back. I never sold my soul to the corporate machine that valued money over doing what was right for the patient. For this, I am forever grateful, and even more grateful for his compassionate wiping away of my daily tears.

INTRODUCTION

It is imperative that I start with a discussion of the state of consciousness in today's corporations. I believe we must start here before we talk about how to survive within a corporation. Understanding the environment you are working in will assist you in trying to navigate it, survive in it, and, if needed, exit it, if it compromises who you are.

Part 1 of this book discusses these issues—specifically, corporate consciousness, how it affects a corporation and its employees, and what it means for everyone. I have also included a discussion on what it means to challenge the status quo.

Part 2 of this book is organized as a series of essays in which each chapter addresses a particular quality necessary to create a positive work environment for employees and employers alike. These qualities function within the scope of ethics and integrity as described in Part 1. Ethics and integrity form the foundation upon which a discussion of these qualities is based.

I've come up with an easy-to-remember acronym for the qualities necessary for a healthy workplace and a successful employee:

H onesty
A chieve
L earn
T rust

Hu mility

R espect

T eamwork   =   **HALT HuRT**

We must take every one of these and make them part of each and every one of us!

Through the use of this acronym, we will, indeed, be able to halt hurt—the hurt experienced by the employee as well as the hurt felt by those whom the employee serves or with whom she or he interacts.

It is important to remember that without ethics and integrity, these qualities will not create a work environment that allows you to achieve success in your job—success measured not only by dollars and cents but by your ability to help create a better world.

These qualities, therefore, should be the core of every working environment to maintain the critical values necessary to practice your trade appropriately, be it medicine, engineering, teaching, manufacturing, or whatever your area of interest and expertise. Maintaining these core values should not impede adhering to the bottom line, the piece that seems so all-consuming to corporate businesses. More will be discussed on these two qualities later on.

By the end of Part 2, you will have insight into a group of qualities that will help you navigate the complexities of working successfully in corporate America, utilizing the core values of ethics and integrity.

Part 3 of this book discusses the trauma of being fired and how to move forward after a termination. This includes allowing yourself to go through the grieving process. I will also describe how to evaluate your options going forward and take advantage of them. These options include the need to reinvent yourself to seek a different line of work or rejoin the workforce in your former capacity. Along with real-life advice, I will provide you with a guide—a road map, so to speak—of how to proceed forward with dignity and grace, and, ultimately, be successful.

Appendix 1 will help you ask the tough questions to get you to think about what we have discussed in this book. The questions will review the qualities necessary to be successful at your job.

Appendix 2 asks questions that will help you to navigate what to do and how to proceed in the event you are fired. These options will be intensively examined. Overall, these questions are designed to help you create a personal road map of where you want to go and how to get there.

One of the important things that you'll learn is there are no right or wrong answers. There are only *your* answers. If you are honest with yourself, you will find your way not only to another job but, more importantly, to a successful, fulfilling career.

There is one last caveat I would like to present before I launch into the specific topics described above. It concerns the difference in the numbers when it comes to men and women being fired.

I did not want to make this book about men versus women. Certainly, there are discrepancies between the genders in the workplace, such as inequality in pay, rates of advancement, and, in some cases, being taken seriously. However, this book is not about these topics—with one exception.
We know for a fact that women are in more danger of being fired than men, In fact, once a woman shatters the glass ceiling, she may find herself standing at a glass precipice.

Why would this be? In some cases, women are hired to take over precarious leadership roles in companies that are faltering in the hope they will engineer a rescue. The reason being, according to Shirley Leung's article that appeared on 10/22/14 in the *Boston Globe* entitled, *"Why do female CEO's get fired more often than male ones?"* women "are perceived to possess traits that are critical in a crisis—the ability to communicate, empathize, and think outside the box."

This is what I believe to be the crux of the problem: "thinking outside the box." Ms. Leung goes on to describe several female CEOs of well-known companies and states "…it may also be because women, not part of the old boys' club, aren't shy about talking out of school…"

Part of what I discuss in this book is being honest, a team player, respecting others, and telling the truth about a situation. Members of the good old boys' club may not be so keen on these traits and view being perceived as leaders via these characteristics, as unorthodox. These can be unfamiliar waters for some men who might not understand the value of these qualities. Or perhaps they feel threatened by them. I'm not certain of the psychology, but I do know it exists.

I do not want to dwell on this more than to bring it to light so we are all aware of this particular inequity. Certainly, it was true in my case—a woman fired by men for being innovative and telling the truth, as I described previously—but it is not everyone's experience. There are plenty of men who get fired for not belonging to the good old boys' club or simply because their integrity and ethics are challenged by the status quo in which they are functioning.

In any case, enough said on this gender-sensitive topic. From this point forward, I want to make sure everyone feels comfortable with the discussions presented.

This topic affects everyone and deserves everyone's attention.

PART 1:

THE CONSCIENCE OF A CORPORATION

CHAPTER ONE: What Does Corporate Consciousness Look Like?

Corporate consciousness—also termed corporate social responsibility (CSR), corporate citizenship, or responsible business—is often described as a self-regulated monitor built into a corporate policy that demonstrates responsibility toward the community. Ways in which corporations exercise corporate consciousness include: contributing to educational and social programs, participating in philanthropy and volunteer activities within their community, promoting ethical marketing and consumerism, and developing environmental policies geared toward waste and pollution reductions.

However, it is important to understand that CSR policies not only extends to the world outside a corporation but that they should also be actively applied internally to the corporate family—the employees.

If we were to agree that this is as important as the social policies extended to the public, employees should be able to ask the corporation they work for or to whom they are applying for work, what their internal CSR is—more specifically, how it is applied to employees. A corporation cannot exclude one from the other without appearing false in its statements.

As an example, imagine that a corporation advertises that it actively participates in philanthropy within its local community as well as in social reform, but its hiring policies are suspect and its treatment of employees is unfair. What would that say about their CSR policy? It certainly demonstrates the true intent of that corporation, suggesting it boasts of its social responsibility platform only so it can increase profits—not because it is the right thing to do.

In fact, when we look at the many definitions of CSR, very few talk about the internal CSR of a corporation. This is important to point out because CSR must have internal and external arms. Employees are not only looking to work within a corporation with outward social responsibility but want to work for a corporation that respects them too.

Therefore, I would like to extend the definition of CSR to include integrity and ethics within the corporate culture, from the CEO to the lowliest employee in the company. A complete CSR policy, then, would describe the internal and external policies a particular corporation adheres too. Such a complete policy would give not only the consumer but also the employee a sense of the "soul" of that corporation.

<u>The Importance of an Internal CSR in the Company You Work for or Want to Work For</u>

We all know that, as consumers, knowing the CSR policies of a company could potentially make a difference in the purchases we make. However, as employees, knowing that a corporation has an internal social policy, indicates that there will be a greater likelihood of fair hiring practices as well as fair internal reviews and probation. It also means that exceptional work performance will be recognized either financially or through corporate advancement. Finally, workplace bullying should also be specifically addressed by corporate leaders.

The lack of an internal CSR policy should make any potential employee wary about the environment they are walking into. Non-existence of an internal CSR policy within a corporation that actively advertises its external CSR policy should make a potential employee run quickly in the opposite direction. Essentially, non-existence of an internal CSR policy means a corporation does not care about anything but a profit, however it is obtained. If you pursue employment with such a corporation, you should know what to expect—a corporation without transparency that may be willing to lie to make a profit and throw you to the wolves, so to speak, as an employee. Be forewarned; such scenarios are not uncommon.

An article in *Journal of Workplace Learning* published by Ferreira and Real de Olivera in February 2014 entitled, *"Does corporate social responsibility impact on employee engagement?"* addresses the above concerns. Another study by Bhattacharya et. al in 2008 in *MIT Sloan Review* entitled *"Using corporate social responsibility to win the war on talent"*, states that companies lacking an internal CSR may face problems in attracting, retaining, and engaging the best employees.

Internal CSRs must address fair working conditions, teamwork, and diversity. The As You Sow Foundation goes further to state that internal CSRs have "management teams that view employees as assets rather than costs."

Asking about a company's CSR policy when applying for a job and the answer you receive will give you a good indication about the health of that corporation and the job satisfaction you may experience working there.

<u>The Relationship Between CSR, the Human Resources Department, and You, the Employee</u>

How does a corporation manage its CSR? The integral tool is the Human Resources (HR) department. However, please understand that just because there is an HR department does not mean there is a healthy internal CSR policy in effect. In some situations, the HR department is simply used as a legal conduit through which to file reports on employees and manage complaints filed about a coworker or management. Therefore, it may not exist as a management tool to help regulate, encourage, and ultimately enforce a CSR policy.

How CSR is linked to HR is described in an article written by Sarah Licha for Linkedin on 6/16/2015 entitled *"Corporate social responsibilty and human resources"*. Here is an excerpt: "Business trends are no longer silos-based, with every department trying to impose supremacy over the others but rather [there's] a tendency aiming at a holistic vision of a well-run company. ...CSR gives rise to a clear company vision and to specific values attached to it. Employees should be able to identify themselves in these values and to share the company's vision. The company should become the employee's DNA... All of the above are HR-related topics and that is why HR has to be involved and consulted on CSR... The company's Code of Conduct and the HR manual are the documents through which a company's commitment to a responsible behavior should be communicated... and the company's commitment to offer an ethical work environment to its employees [is relayed]... Remember, employees who are committed are the company's best ambassadors."

Just to be clear, the responsible behaviors associated with internal CSR and regulated by HR would include but certainly not be limited to: defined confidentiality agreements, protection of intellectual property, appropriate use of emails, intolerance of harassment (bullying or disrespect at the workplace), protection for whistleblowing, a definition of what is considered appropriate in terms of gifts, and intolerance of nepotism and corruption (bribes).

These are important concepts to understand as we continue to discuss later on, the relationship between an internal CSR and what it means to you as an employee.
In essence, transparency of the HR department is a crucial factor for anyone considering employment at a company. Certainly, all employees should be given an HR manual at the time of their employment. It is imperative that a future employee review this document, paying careful attention to the tenor of what is said and determining if and how appropriate behaviors are encouraged, what are considered inappropriate behaviors and how these behaviors are addressed.

CHAPTER TWO: The Argument Against Corporate Consciousness

There are many articles stating that corporate social responsibility, or, as some call it, "conscious capitalism," is an oxymoron. In other words, you cannot have both consciousness and capitalism operating at once. Of course, capitalism is based on a free market, with an emphasis on corporations realizing the most profit and consumers getting the best deals possible.

However, nowhere in these definitions does it state that, in capitalism, the ends are more important than the means. This has been the implied belief of many corporations, a belief that is meeting its demise as the world becomes a village and people can see the immediate results on workers' rights and the environment of doing business solely for a profit. One only has to look to recent news releases concerning poor factory work conditions, child labor, and environmental disasters to understand the impact that such tragic stories have on public opinion and how that might influence buyers' choices.

An example of the influence of public opinion is the choices women are beginning to make about the cosmetics they buy—choices not only based on the quality of these products but whether animal testing—i.e., animal cruelty—is involved in their production.

The argument for corporate conscience has extended to include such ideas as corporate moral responsibility and whether a corporation can be held accountable to these concepts as if it were an individual—in other words, whether a corporation is considered, legally, to be a person in this regard.

As per an article in *Harvard Business Review* in 1982 by Goodpaster and Mathews entitled *"Can a corporation have a conscience"*, "legally, a corporation can be considered a unit." The authors go on to state that "corporations that monitor their employment practices and the effects of their production processes and products on the environment and human health show the same kind of rationality and respect that morally responsible individuals do. Thus, attributing actions, strategies, decisions and moral responsibilities to corporations as entities distinguishable from those who hold offices in them poses no problem."

The line starts to blur when corporations include religious beliefs as part of their moral base. A *New York Times* article by Timothy Egan that appeared on April 3, 2015 entitled *"The conscience of a corporation"*, talks about the religion-based discrimination reflected in some corporate policies and whether these would be considered at odds with what Walmart claims is its "core basic belief of respect for the individual." However, as Egan states, "you can blame last year's Supreme Court decision in the Hobby Lobby case for unleashing a herd of ponies that have gone off in quite unpredicted directions. There…the court gave certain corporations the right to challenge laws that they claim violate their religious beliefs. In that case, it was about contraception in the [employee] healthcare package."

So, it might seem simple to come up with clear-cut policies involving internal as well as external CSR, but, in reality, belief systems often prevail and the waters become muddied when trying to please everyone.

This same article goes on to state that the importance of internal CSR in corporate America has been reduced to "the branding conceit of the moment including just the right dash of social activism. A little environmental nudge from your cereal, a talk about race from your barista—it's mostly harmless." This is an unfortunate state of affairs in today's marketplace, but there is hope. As Mackey and Sisodia stated in a 2013 *Harvard Business Review* article entitled, *"Conscious capitalism is not an oxymoron,"* "There is a growing network of people—including the leaders of companies such as Container Store, Starbucks, Trader Joe's, Patagonia, and Whole Foods Market—building their companies based on business practices we have come to call 'conscious capitalism.' Every year, we come in contact with more leaders who share the same beliefs."

So, as you look at the corporation where you already work or are hoping to be hired, these concepts are important for you, as an employee, to understand and ask questions about. It is no longer appropriate for a company to dismiss corporate consciousness as an oxymoron and use it as an excuse for promoting an external CSR platform when there is no internal CSR.

As for internal CSR, more and more corporations are looking inward at the environment they have created for their employees. Respect for employees, value given for team work, and intolerance of bullying are major factors in the functionality of a corporation, and addressing these can only bring that corporation better profits. Employees are much more likely to work together for the common product if they feel valued and respected as individuals.

The validity of such an attitude was written about by Tony Schwartz of the *Harvard Business Review* in an article that appeared on April 4, 2013 entitled, *"Companies that practice conscious capitalism perform 10X better."* As the title indicates, the assumption that a happy worker equals a happy company has been proven many times over. The article states, "Raj Sisodia, a business professor, looked at 28 companies he identified as the most conscious...based on characteristics such as their stated purpose, generosity of compensation, quality of customer service, investment in their communities, and impact on the environment. The 18 publicly traded companies out of the 28 outperformed the S&P 500 index by a factor of 10.5 over the years 1996-2011. The more conscious companies give more and they get more in return.

The inescapable conclusion: it pays to care, widely and deeply."

CHAPTER THREE: Ask Not What The Corporation Can Do for You, But What You Can Do for The Corporation

In the previous two chapters, I reviewed how CSR was defined and manifested, the aspects of CSR, and how these characteristics benefit not only the community in which the company operates but the individuals within these corporations.

Let's put a different spin on the discussion. Let's talk about what you, as the individual employee, can do for the corporation you work for or will eventually work for.

"Wait, what?" you say. "I need to ask what I can do for *them*?" Actually, yes, because corporate consciousness is based on equity; it's not a singular responsibility. You need the company to provide you with a "job," maybe even a "career." For the purposes of this discussion, it really doesn't matter if you view the company as a stepping stone or a career choice. However, whatever the reason you work for that particular company, you must realize that organization needs you just as much or more than you need it—not only for success in its business sector but to be in compliance with its internal CSR policies.

Let me give you some simple examples.

Imagine that, as an employee, you are labeled a bully, disrespectful toward others, dishonest, and not a team player. Your activity within the corporation may decrease morale, cause others to leave, and negatively affect overall productivity, which impacts profits.

If on the other hand, you have been a model employee as identified in the internal CSR policies such as being a team player, praising others as appropriate, respecting others' opinions, and helping others feel valued, you would be a tremendous asset to that company. You would have allowed the corporation to maintain its internal CSR, improve morale, increase retention of its employees, and, hopefully, increase productivity.

Which employee do you think a corporation would want to have working for them? The answer is obvious, right?

"Okay", you say, "but in my case, it doesn't matter. I work for a corporation without an internal CSR policy, so my behavior does not impact the health of the company." This situation is a little trickier to navigate. Despite your company not having such a policy, your continued example of how an employee behaving *as if* there were an internal CSR policy may help that company look more closely at your positive behavior and the overall impact it has on profits. Even if the initial attention is on the increased profits that result from such behavior, eventually that company may look at all the benefits and look toward adopting policies that encourage and even reward such behavior.

Of course, this last example may currently be unobtainable within the company in which you work. Either management doesn't care or it feels that the increase in profits would be minimal if an internal CSR were established, or the behavior you are trying to emulate so that others start acting similarly is shut down by bullying or in other ways.

Perhaps, you feel you are putting yourself at risk of getting fired by trying to act in accordance with CSR policies present in other companies. That is certainly possible. As one of the Republican candidates for the 2016 presidential bid, Carly Fiorina, said when asked about getting fired as the CEO of Hewlett Packard, "I challenged the status quo, so I was fired." Her statement inspired the title of this book.

This is really the essence of what I want to present to you, the reader. Challenging the status quo implies that the status quo does not include Corporate Social Responsibility, internal and/or external. I will explore this topic further in the next chapter. Challenging the status quo or not, just remember that when there is no CSR, the risk to employees includes getting fired.

Employers would be wise to consider CSR as real and necessary for the health of their company. Eventually, it may be needed as a legal protection. Employees, despite the potential risk of getting fired, should insist on an internal CSR policy if none exist.

And, as difficult as it may be to insist on this—especially for you, the individual employee, who feels at risk for being fired—please understand that your mental if not physical health as well as the health of your career depend on working within an organization that values you as a person and an employee. In return, you must value the corporation for what it represents to its employees as well as its community.

So, with all this said, before I continue to describe in detail what qualities are necessary to function well within an environment that supports internal CSR, let's take a look at what challenging the status quo really means.

CHAPTER 4: Challenging the Status Quo: Perspectives From Employers and Employees

Wise bosses have the confidence to act on what they know and the humility to doubt their knowledge.
Bob Sutton

The manager accepts the status quo; the leader challenges it.
Warren G. Bennis

From the standpoint of an employer who feels that "things are working as is, why change" or "don't change something that is not broken", employees that challenge the status quo pose a dilemma. The dilemma stems from the fear that the leader of the organization, be it the boss, the manager or the CEO, will lose credibility as knowing what's best for their company, based on his or hers experience and/or knowledge base.

However, that fear is completely unfounded in the eyes of the employees, who instead, look for a leader who is willing to accept new ideas and is capable of initiating innovative change that will continue to grow that company to ensure continued success. This success directly translates to employees who feel as part of the team that is critical to the company's success and therefore feel fulfilled in their jobs.

What qualities do those in leadership display that allows there to be challenges to the status quo? Certainly, keeping an open mind and understanding that change is inevitable are critical to any leader willing to continuously grow and transform their organization.

The opposite, to remain in the status quo, equals stagnation, i.e., no growth. It represents the possibility of going backward instead of forward, if those working in that environment are stuck with a set of rules that worked previously but are now in fact, outdated.

How can you determine if a company you are considering to be hired in or one that you already work at, has leadership that values change?

Attempt to observe whether the leaders of that company seem to embrace change. How can you do this? Find out if they ask employees for fresh ideas. Ask the current employees if their bosses listen to their opinions. Do they respect those with fresh ideas or are they scoffed at? Are the bosses willing to make mistakes and not blame their employees, so they can learn better ways on how to reach the goals they are seeking? Or if failure ensues, do the employees face the consequences.

In addition, look at the mission statement of that company. Their "why" should be part of the culture of moving forward. The "why" cannot exist if a company is unwilling to change to accommodate the "what" and "how" you need to achieve the "why" with.

Finally, as I discussed in the previous chapter, knowing that a company has an internal corporate social responsibility will facilitate leadership encouraging the status quo to be challenged without fear of being fired.

An example of this follows.

Imagine a company that manufactures wheelchairs. What would be the "why " of that company? I would venture to say it would be "to provide the best mobility to those needing help so that life is lived to the fullest". Right?

Ok. So imagine that a new technology comes along that allows a patient without mobility, to walk again. This technology would surpass the capability of being wheelchair bound.

Remember, that the "why" not only includes providing mobility but also includes the statement "to live life to the fullest".

The company CEO can respond in one of two ways.

A CEO that wants to keep the status quo would say, "wheelchairs provide mobility, there is no need to improve on a product that is not broken or faulty". That CEO would pass on the chance to manufacture the new technology because "nothing is broken, leave well enough alone". Most likely, a company with this leadership would not be interested in any of their employees challenging this line of thought.

An innovative CEO, would instead jump at the chance to embrace this new technology. The "why" that further extends to "live life to the fullest" would strike a chord and producing this new technology would only enhance their product line and fulfill the "why" initially stated. Employees who work for this CEO would help accomplish this by presenting fresh approaches to launching this innovative technology to improve mobility and the CEO would listen. In the scenario that involves the CEO who embraces change, not only will patients benefit from this new product line, but the company will indeed be compensated with increased sales and lauded as innovative in the face of an otherwise stagnant marketplace for wheelchairs and walkers.

With this example, you can also see that not only does the company benefit with increased sales, but also individuals and society as a whole reap the rewards of an innovative idea being embraced. Truly a win-win for all sides.

So, whether you are looking from within, at the company you work for, or outward, looking for a job, it would behoove you to take to heart the importance of challenging the status quo. In addition, this is a trait or quality you want to see a company embrace, not steer away from. You want to see a company encourage its employees to challenge the status quo, with the goal to better themselves and as a result, better the community.

Finding anything less will leave you filling empty, unsatisfied and quickly bored with the work you do. Perhaps it will pay the bills, but again, at what cost to your physical and mental health.

Change is inevitable, my friend. As hard as that concept may be to embrace, you need to be able to do so. To only expect or accept the status quo, will leave you empty of the joy of living life to the fullest and making a difference along the way.

PART 2:

QUALITIES NECESSARY FOR YOU TO SURVIVE AND THRIVE

The first part of this book described the benefits of Corporate Social Responsibility (CSR) within an organization, including internal and external policies. It also reviewed what challenging the status quo really means, what it looks like and how an internal CSR supports this concept.

Below, I want to help you, the employee, navigate how to participate and behave within this CSR, specifically the internal portion. Although each corporation will differ in minor points, the overall traits needed to be successful are presented with examples and worksheets provided to help you develop each quality to the fullest.

CHAPTER ONE: H is for HONESTY

"Honesty is the first chapter in the book of Wisdom."
Thomas Jefferson

Let's examine the definition of honesty.

As per Merriam-Webster, honesty is, *fairness and straightforwardness of conduct. Adherence to the facts; sincerity.*

Here is my personal experience of honesty:

I walked into the subspecialty unit where I worked one morning and found two other subspecialists from two different areas, waiting for me.

"Let's be honest here, Cristina," one doctor said as soon as he saw me. "You and I both know this patient should have been transferred to this facility much sooner than today, right?" The other doctor nodded his head.

And so my day started with trying to find out what had happened while at the same time trying to do what was needed to help this patient survive. I succeeded in one of these endeavors. I did find out what had happened, but I failed improving the outcome of our patient, despite the aggressive treatments we tried.

What led to this poor outcome? Honesty had been missing in this scenario since before the patient arrived.

Let's look at how this happened.

Essentially, the physician at the transferring hospital had not been honest with the patient's family. He did not tell them that the appropriate subspecialists were at a different hospital, where the patent would receive better treatment. His omission of this fact as well as allowing the family to believe that the initial hospital could do everything the hospital with specialized care could do, constituted dishonesty.

The family knew we had done everything possible to improve this patient's outcome. They finally understood, after seeing the advanced technology and therapeutics used to help this patient survive, that indeed the capabilities of the other hospital were limited.

I brought this case to my peers to evaluate, discuss, and learn from. I did not want this scenario to ever happen again, with any physician.

You might ask, was it malicious dishonesty on the part of the other physician and his team? I do not believe so. Look again at what Thomas Jefferson wrote: "Honesty is the first chapter in the book of wisdom." I simply think this physician, as the leader of his team, lacked the wisdom to be able to be honest with himself or the patient's family. Unfortunately, the compounding factor was that this lack of wisdom co-existed with the physician's arrogance. That combination led to the undesirable outcome of this patient.

As one of my mentor physicians once told me during fellowship, "A great physician knows their limit." That is so true, and, oftentimes, so under-practiced.

Dishonesty in Other Aspects of Life

This is but one example of many and certainly not exclusive to the world of medicine. We don't have to look very far to see how dishonesty is often a deciding factor in an outcome.

Let's look at examples outside the medical arena. Honesty in business is vital. A perfect example is the real-estate crash that happened a few years back, which was coupled with the dishonest behavior of the banks foreclosing on properties without giving ample warning to homeowners. What ensued was not only devaluation of homes and a bursting of the dishonest, over-inflated housing bubble but also the improper eviction of hundreds of homeowners without so much as a month's notice. These banks were eventually found guilty and fined. They were supposed to return money to these homeowners, but few ever saw a settlement and, for those that did, the amounts awarded were pitiful. Dishonesty was abundant, both in the real estate market and the banking industry, but there were no other consequences for the perpetrators. The banks survived, but many homeowners are, to this day, struggling to pay their mortgage, in default, or worse—declaring bankruptcy.

Shall I even talk about honesty or the lack thereof in politics? I think not! I imagine you could readily identify some astonishing examples from the current headline news.

So, how do we tackle this problem of lack of honesty in the workplace?

No doubt this is a difficult question with an even more difficult answer.

For employers, honesty includes being truthful to employees concerning their work performance, project management, or taking time off. As an employee, your honesty is reflected in your work ethic. Just as you do not want your boss to abuse your work relationship through bullying, dishonest evaluations, or unfair work practices, you should not show poor work ethics by using your position or taking advantage of coworkers to benefit yourself. You should be sincere in talking with clients but share only the facts of the business transaction, whether that involves a work-order, a contract, or other related business. Overstating or exaggerating what you, as a business, can do for a client may get you the job or contract, but, eventually, this dishonesty will backfire when the client does not receive what was promised.

In the medical world, honesty is the best policy when the time comes to discuss with a patient or a patient's family issues concerning care, risks, and prognosis, no matter how difficult those discussions might be.

The Foundation of Honesty—Being Honest with Yourself

Most importantly, in any situation, being honest with yourself concerning your capabilities and/or your actions precedes what you present to others. Essentially, if you are not honest with yourself, you will never be able to be honest with others.

Sometimes, honesty is difficult. It may be painful for the person you are being honest with. "No, that was not your best work; No, I do not like your presentation, your idea, your drawings, your book; No, you are not looking well; This cancer will be hard to treat and we may not be successful; etc."

I am sure you have been in difficult scenarios in which you wished you did not have to be honest. It seemed that dishonesty would be less painful. Perhaps, in the short-term, it would. But, in the long-term, your dishonesty takes on a life of its own and the negative effects multiply to eventually be more damaging than the initial pain of being honest.

"The least initial deviation from the truth is multiplied later a thousand fold." Aristotle

<u>Responding to Dishonesty in Others</u>

Encountering dishonesty is an even more difficult problem to tackle. Who do you tell?
Do you confide in another coworker? Do you tell your boss? Do you confront the person being dishonest?

The best policy—and one I had to remind myself of constantly—is to confront the person directly before going to anyone else. This is difficult to do because you anticipate the reaction of the person you are talking to may be anger. Confrontation is never easy. If after talking with that person, he or she remains obstinate and will not own up to their dishonesty—whether because of ignorance and being unwilling to learn a better way or because of malicious behavior—it is time to act. You will need to step up and, armed with facts, talk to your boss or supervisor.
Never talk about that person to another coworker. That amounts to gossip and ends up being harmful, accomplishing nothing.

Once you have taken your concerns up the ladder, so to speak, let those in charge take over.

What if those in charge do nothing or slide your concerns under the table, protecting the person who was dishonest because they are otherwise good performers and therefore good for the company? Well, now you have a problem. In some cases, you can take your concerns to an even higher level. However, there might not be a higher level, or that higher level may do the same thing and hide the truth.

At this point, you have a decision to make. Is the dishonesty of a critical nature or mostly insignificant and unlikely to affect other individuals or the company? Is it something you can live with? If the answer to these questions is no, you must decide if it is time to move on and find another job.

I certainly know this is easier said than done.
In fact, that was my case. Even though I brought this medical case to my peers and superiors and they reviewed it and agreed with me, the consequence was a "slap on the hand" to the other physician and a warning not to do it again. Was there any teaching, mentoring, or probation period? No.

It was difficult for me to live with this, but I had no other choice because of my contract. There was no job I could transfer to. My only saving grace was knowing I would continue to do everything I could for the patients under my care and try to make a difference in their outcome. It was not the best solution, but it was a compromise I could live with.

I agree with Thomas Jefferson about honesty being the cornerstone of wisdom. These are certainly sage words to live by. Without honesty, everything collapses. You cannot build a strong foundation at your work without honesty as the essential building block. Trust cannot follow without honesty, nor can respect, both of which are essential components of success as a person, a teammate, an office or factory worker, a manager, or a leader.

"Whoever is careless with the truth in small matters cannot be trusted with important matters." Albert Einstein

Never forget this.

CHAPTER TWO- A is for ACHIEVE

"A dream becomes a goal when action is taken toward its achievement." Bo Bennett

The definition of "achieve" as per Merriam-Webster is: *To get or reach something by working hard. To reach a goal.*

Here is my personal experience:

A few years back, in 2008, to be exact, a subspecialist from another area with whom I was working with, came to my office shortly after returning from a conference in her subspecialty. "Cristina," she said, "I just learned about this new and exciting treatment for patients that have suffered from a certain disease process. We should look into it and see if you could apply it to your patients.

"Wow!" I said. "What you are describing sounds really cool. Let me look into it and I'll give you a call."

That day, I started looking into this new treatment modality and, within half a year, the other subspecialist and I had created a protocol that was approved by the appropriate committees within our hospital. Our first patient had this innovative treatment done in the summer of 2008. From that point forward, we were able to provide this aggressive, innovative therapy and significantly improve long term outcomes in that particular population. Since its inception, we have had six annual reunions of all the graduates of this program; published several abstracts and a peer-reviewed paper; and received many accolades from the community.

Our dream project generated a goal of treating all patients with this specific disease, by being transported to our specialized unit, thereby achieving the best long-term outcomes possible. Our goal became a reality.

"Great," you say. "What is the problem? You set a goal and achieved it. What more can I learn about this quality, the need to achieve? It's obvious how to do this, right? You identify a problem, look for a solution, and move forward to implement that solution."

Well, in fact, there is more to this than just identifying a problem and moving forward to create a solution to bring a dream to reality. Your dream of solving a problem must be a collective dream that everyone you work with agrees with and wants to be a part of. Without the buy-in from all or the majority of your coworkers, it will be an uphill battle to prove that, indeed, this dream is important and necessary for everyone to participate in to achieve the success you're striving for.

That was my mistake—not getting buy-in from people lateral to me and making everyone a partner in the process of creating this unique unit. Although the ancillary healthcare workers who worked with me had also bought into the project and were quite excited about it, as were my superiors, my partners—those lateral to me—were not. Therefore, I received little support from them and, in fact, the reverse happened. They became jealous of the results we were obtaining and even more jealous of the attention the media showered on our team.

Paul Ryan said it well: *"Every successful individual knows that his or her achievement depends on a community of persons working together."*

Even though the community of ancillary healthcare workers—nurses, nurse practitioners and other subspecialists - were part of the dynamic team that bought into our dream, my physician partners were not part of this dream or team. They felt so disenfranchised, that statements were made alluding to the possibility I had fudged the data to make our achievements that much more exciting.

Lesson learned. Involve everyone in your dream. Allow everyone to be an active participant to make it a reality and achieve success. Make sure everyone feels themselves to be an integral part of this dream, of the process, and of the success obtained.

By team I don't only mean the group of people working with you. I mean those who are part of the bigger picture in your group, whether they are the other members of your team or your company as a whole, no matter how big that company is. Both Microsoft and Apple offer a great example of this inclusion. There may be a few individuals who create the dreams that move forward to become realities, but the whole company supports and celebrates the achieved success because everyone is made to feel they were an integral part of the process.

"Great players are willing to give up their own personal achievement for the achievement of the group. It enhances everyone." Kareem Abdul-Jabbar.

Well said, and this applies not only to sports but to every achievement sought by a single individual with the help of others. Remember, you cannot achieve your dream alone. Just like it takes a village to raise a child, it takes a whole team to achieve success.

Another important concept that further describes how to achieve success is described in the important book, *Start with Why,* by Simon Sinek. In this book, Sinek explains that the ability to achieve success is found when the question "why?" is asked. Why is what you are working on important for your company, group, or project? When the "why" is answered, the how to go about making it a reality becomes evident. I highly recommend that you take a closer look at this concept. Mr. Sinek's book is informative and the knowledge it contains should become a permanent part of your inner repertoire of strategies to move forward.

Using all these pointers will help you in your quest to achieve success and become an integral part of the bigger picture—the company or group you are working in or with.

Finally, wanting to achieve success and making this desire a part of your daily mantra is critically important for your survival within your company or group. Without it, you will be less apt to be a team player and less apt to want to build, explore, create, and find new ways of doing things and making progress. Without this important quality—the desire to achieve success—the status quo will always be enough. In fact, challenging the status quo will become a mute point. Stagnation, therefore, becomes the norm, and no one strives for a brighter, better future.

CHAPTER THREE: L Is for LEARNING

"Being ignorant is not so much a shame as being unwilling to learn." Benjamin Franklin

"I am still learning." Michelangelo

The definition of the word "learn" in Merriam-Webster is: *To gain knowledge, understanding, or skill by study, instruction, or experience.*

Franklin and Michelangelo were two of the greatest thinkers and inventors of all time. Despite their greatness, both stated they continued to learn, always. To think we no longer need to learn is arrogant. There is another caveat to this. If you believe you are still learning, you must also accept that someone needs to teach you. This means someone knows something you do not.

Is this a shameful state of affairs? Of course not. No one would believe this to be true. Yet, some people, when challenged with not knowing something, feel they do not need to be taught. This is especially true of professionals such as physicians. Doctors are notorious for believing we know it all and should never be challenged—by patients, family members, or other physicians. Maybe that is because we are made to feel we are elite members of society when we are accepted into medical school. That feeling of elitism can prevail throughout medical school, residency, and onward into the chosen career path. Curriculums today at some medical schools are starting to address this by admitting it exists and finding ways to neutralize it. No one should ever feel they are above others, above learning continuously and above respecting everyone for their individual talents and/or the roles they play to make the team work seamlessly.

Here is my personal experience:

My former physician colleagues had accused me of being a "know-it-all" in the unit I worked in. Yet, it was because I was willing to challenge our team and learn a new technology and treatment modality, that we were able to provide this advanced and innovative therapy to those patients who needed it the most.

When I first heard about it, I had no idea such therapy existed, but I was so excited to learn and implement it for the benefit of patients who needed it. Even after we were successfully initiating this new treatment, questions we could not answer arose frequently. These questions continued to challenge me and our team to find answers. I did not know everything, nor had I ever claimed I did. What I did was challenge others to understand what we were doing—the "why" of it, as I explained in the last chapter: Why was this therapy so important and necessary for certain patients?

I invited my colleagues to come visit and see what we were doing, i.e., to learn from our team. Alas, these invites fell on deaf ears. They would not listen to the "whys," no matter how much I tried to teach them. Instead, our unit continued to be criticized, a criticism aimed at all the healthcare workers involved, and, most intensely, at me. I was accused of being insistent on describing the unit we created as a center of excellence, which our detractors did not believe it was. Yet, they never came to see for themselves whether it was or not.

Their opinions were formed by the belief they could not learn anything new and they knew the best way of treating patients.

In another example, we had recently learned that one of the drugs we had been using for many years to treat a particular illness was actually harmful to certain cells in the body over long-term usage. When this was brought up at one of our conferences, one physician stated, "Oh, of course. Now you are telling me we have been hurting the very patients we were trying to help all these years." In reality, we did not know about this when we were prescribing that particular drug. But now we did. We learned something new, which meant we needed to change our mode of treating this disease. Instead of embracing this, the initial response was to accuse me of stating we were deliberately harming our past patients.

I must say, I was totally unprepared for these responses and criticisms. I thought we had all taken the Hippocratic Oath, in which we swore to do the best for each patient, always, and that we would do no harm. What happened? Why were there obstacles to instituting new therapies? Why was the answer to the question "why?" not embraced?

I have to admit, I was passionate about what my team and I were doing for these patients. I wanted everyone to be excited and share in the successes of each and every patient that benefited from it. So, when I started to encounter unfounded criticism, I responded with my own criticism. I had tried to teach; we had done outreach and presented data, yet we continued to meet resistance.

I, in turn, felt the need to defend what we were doing. Initially, my defense consisted of continually trying to educate. However, when I met ongoing resistance, I started to lash out. I did this vocally within my group by attacking their failure to keep current on knowledge in the field and their resistance to learn what we were trying to teach.

Everyone who knows me knows I am a patient teacher. But if I feel that I am being ridiculed or am unfairly criticized, I will respond. My response? "I cannot tolerate ignorance or people who refuse to learn—in other words, ignorant people." As you, the reader, can imagine, that did not endear me to anyone within my group that had been resistant to not only embracing new knowledge but even making the effort to learn about it.

How did I know I was being ridiculed, you might ask? I was asked to present our innovative treatment to our group, by my physician "protector" during our weekly group meeting. While I was making my presentation, several members of my group, who were sitting in the back, began snickering and smirking as I spoke.

That was the beginning of my struggle to try to bring this new information to our group. This ridicule never stopped. In fact, after a few months, I was asked to again review our new treatment modality with the group, since it had continued to evolve. However, it was evident there was a continued lack of support for this modality based on the fact that patients who would most benefit, were not being transferred to our unit. Out of the many members of our group, only two physicians showed up for my presentation. I had, in effect, been boycotted.

There was no further improvement in this situation. A subsequent meeting of other physicians in our group who were in charge of their respective units at other hospitals, resulted in a stalemate.

Excuses for Unwillingness to Learn

You can see examples of unwillingness to learn or the "know-it-all" attitude all around you. You see it in the unwillingness to change "what isn't broken." This is code language for "We have been doing it the same way for a long time, and it's worked, so why change?" It is also code for, "I'm comfortable with the way I do things and I do not want to change."

Change is very scary. Change goes against the flow and implies you need to learn something new, which goes back to the implication you didn't know everything in the first place. This stream of thought progresses to not being seen as an expert or a leader, because now you are being told you need to learn something new and change.

All these reasons—fear of being seen as behind the times, fear of losing the qualifications of a leader or an expert, and fear of having to change one's routine—come between the ego and the willingness to learn and improve. Unwillingness to accept the need to change makes businesses stagnant and stifles creativity.

How to Respond to Unwillingness to Learn

So, how can you, the reader, circumvent issues such as these? Great question and, guess what. I'm still learning!

Perhaps patience is the best answer. Even when meeting resistance, try to bring others into the fold and ask what they are resistant to in terms of what you are trying to teach. Ask what would make them feel more enthusiastic about learning something new. Ask how you could present the information better.

You may do all of this and still be met with significant, obstinate resistance. Then what?
You might need to enlist the help of others who are not seen as your equal but are seen as experts in the field. In other words, bring in someone who is well-respected in the field to talk to the group of professionals you are trying to teach.

If all else fails, continue to do the best work you can, and continue to teach when you are able and when you are invited to. Do not become frustrated. That just leads to more feelings of resentment, not only in you but in others. These feelings bring the learning process to an immediate halt.

The attitude of the individuals in the group of people you are trying to teach will determine how successful you will be. Perhaps the following says it all:

"I am always ready to learn although I do not always like being taught." Winston Churchill

In my case, the situation never improved and, therefore, my criticism of others continued and increased. I could not tolerate ignorance, and I paid the price. Don't let this happen to you. Quit if you feel you are not achieving your goal, but do not compromise your health, physical or mental, because of the stress generated by lack of support from others. Eventually, the old ways will fall by the wayside and the new will become the norm until the next learning curve becomes necessary. The sooner this learning curve is embraced by everyone, the sooner progress occurs, and, in fact, that progress will exponentially escalate. After a while, that company or that technology will catch up. Others will start to see that the new norm is no longer stagnation but growth through learning. You may not be around to see this or be vindicated, but it will happen. That is the way the world works—life continues to evolve.

CHAPTER FOUR: T is for TRUST

"Whoever is careless with the truth in small matters cannot be trusted with important matters." Albert Einstein

"Trust is the glue of life. It's the most essential ingredient in effective communication. It is the foundational principle that holds all relationships." Stephen Covey

Trust is defined by Merriam-Webster as: *Assured reliance on the character, ability, strength, or truth of someone or something.*

Are there any "truer" statements than these? I think not!

In all areas of life, truth or having the ability to trust another is so important. When we are dealing with life-and-death matters, as is frequently the case in medicine, trust is essential. Without it, patient care would be so negatively impacted that it would be safer to go to a shaman to be healed.

I think that, although honesty is intimately tied to trust, you could possibly experience one without the other. Let me give you some personal examples.

<u>Trust without honesty:</u>

I walked into a local medical conference one day and saw one of my colleagues who had a practice at another facility. He was well-respected, knowledgeable, and I trusted his knowledge base. We started talking and he told me about a patient he had at his facility that developed a complication.

While listening to him, I believed the patient might have a better chance of full recovery with a better long-term outcome, if that patient were transferred to another facility. When I suggest this to him, he told me that the patient was getting all the care needed at his facility and therefore did not need to be moved.

I later found out that the family had already requested the patient be moved, but this same physician told them there was no need because his facility provided the same care as the one the family requested.

So, in this instance, although I trusted my colleague's knowledge, he was not truthful with himself or with the patient's family concerning the care the patient was receiving. In other words, he had developed trust within the medical community as a knowledgeable physician but he was dishonest about the care this particular patient and similar patients were receiving.

Honesty without trust:

At another hospital, I used to know a physician who was brutally honest with families concerning their loved ones chances of living or dying. However, many of us did not trust her medical assessments nor believed she was doing everything possible to change the odds in favor of her patient's survival. She would state to the patient's family that the patient was so sick that death was imminent. In her mind, she was being honest. However, her mediocre medical knowledge in certain situations made her untrustworthy.

These are but two small examples within the field of medicine. A few similar situations in other professions are further described.

For instance, it may be difficult to find out the conditions of workers in a developing country where the manufacture of a particular company's clothing is outsourced. The company, instead, might boast of the low cost of their clothes as their way of helping families survive in today's economy but may not be willing to openly share with the public the truth concerning why those clothes are so cheap to purchase.

Another example is a food company that honestly claims its animal products—eggs, for example—are organic but the company is not truthful about the inhumane living conditions of the animals producing these products.

And so, you can see how you can have one without the other. You can also find, more frequently, neither aspect—trust nor honesty—exist in a company. Less frequently you will be able to find both. Of course, the former situation is of utmost concern. In such cases, both the integrity and ethics of a company are compromised.

So, how do you address these issues?
First and foremost, both of these conditions—trust and honesty—must co-exist if you are working in an office, factory, company, hospital, school, etc., to ensure you are working in an ethical environment.

Which brings us to another concept—ethical behavior. I did not separate this one out because, obviously, to be ethical, you must be honest and truthful. Ethical behavior demands

CRISTINA CARBALLO-PERELMAN, M.D.

that everyone exhibit these traits. Those around you who do not, imperil that business, practice, or organization. White-collar crime is an example of unethical practice that results from these two entities not existing together.

What Are Your Options if You Witness Unethical Behavior?

If you see unethical behavior where you work, you must be able to bring this to a higher-level person in the company or organization. If you see or know that dishonesty, corruption, or unethical behavior continues up the chain to the top, there is no other option except to leave. To do otherwise will compromise your personal integrity and risk your professional life forever, and it may even implicate you in possible criminal activity.

These are difficult issues to address. In today's economy, it is difficult to leave a job that may pay well or that may give you great experience or recommendations to continue to climb the corporate ladder. But do you really want to participate in unethical or criminal activity? Even if you are never "caught," will you truly enjoy the benefits your salary provides? Will you enjoy climbing the corporate ladder, a ladder that is corrupt?

There is no solution other than leaving the organization and seeking employment elsewhere. Be honest with both the company you left and with those who ask you why you left. That does not mean you need to tell others about unethical practices. You simply need to state that you and your employer did not see eye to eye concerning its business practices, and that remaining in that workplace made you feel uncomfortable. If you are asked for details, you direct the person asking, to speak to your employer. Unless you are prepared to go to appropriate authorities with hard evidence—if, for instance, you suspect criminal activity—remove yourself from the situation and simply state the facts as noted above. Eventually, if there is a problem, it will be discovered.

However, what if what is happening at the company is hurting others or criminal in nature? Again, you must be willing to go to appropriate authorities with hard evidence and be prepared to go through significant interrogation until the truth is discovered. Without hard evidence, you could possibly be slapped with a slander lawsuit. It could get ugly. You do not want to go down that road. Again, if evidence is clear and abundant, by all means, present it to whoever you need to, that will allow appropriate action to be taken. You will need to make that call as to how best to proceed.

CHAPTER 5: Hu Is for HUMILITY

"The first test of a truly great man is his humility. By humility, I don't mean doubt of his powers or hesitation in speaking his opinion, but merely an understanding of the relationship of what he can say and what he can do." John Ruskin

"I always say be humble but be firm. Humility and openness are the keys to success without compromising your beliefs." George Hickenlooper

"Have the humility to learn from those around you." John C. Maxwell

Humility, as defined by Merriam-Webster, is as follows: *The quality or state of not thinking you are better than other people.*

These quotes and definition bring home the message that humility is not the same as ignorance. Humility means knowing you don't know everything; you are willing to learn—not begrudgingly, but with grace. Humility means you cannot disrespect the teacher, because that person brings new knowledge you did not have. Humility allows you to learn with grace and gratitude.

Here is my personal experience:

I have already shared with you my attempts to teach my colleagues about a new treatment strategy for patients at risk for poor long-term outcomes. I told you the responses I received—smirks, being completely ignored, and even being told I fudged data showing that this particular treatment strategy was successful.

I was called the opposite of humble—arrogant—because of my zeal to have everyone buy in to this new treatment strategy. However, they mistook passion about a new technology I LEARNED for arrogance. I was humble, not only by stating I needed to learn something new and wanting to teach others for the purpose of benefiting patients, but also because I always emphasized I was part of a team, i.e., I kept in mind the bigger picture. I never said I knew it all—that *would* be arrogance. I was quite clear that I was still learning, because there are always additional questions that surfaced as we learned more about medical advances. Yet, others did not see this. They were so arrogant in the belief they knew everything (how could *anyone* teach them something new?) that they shut me out.

I can see in other workplace scenarios that humility might be viewed as being wimpy, noncommittal, less involved, or simply stupid. As an example, imagine if Mother Teresa had not been taken seriously because others focused on her humility rather than her organizational skill to mobilize her missionary group to do works of charity. Imagine if Steve Jobs had not been taken seriously because of his humble beginnings, starting his company from within a garage and never finishing college? What would the world have lost in just these two examples had both these important people— who changed the world as we know it, in different ways— been ignored for being humble?

So, how do you handle this, if it happens to you? It's more useful to ask ourselves, "How could I have handled the situation better?" Using my experience with resistant colleagues might help answer this question. First, we must let go of our frustration with other people's arrogant ignorance. Okay, that feels better, right? Remind yourself that their thinking needs to be channeled into believing that their learning something new doesn't challenge their arrogance! Wow, that's a clever trick! In other words, try to teach them without them realizing that is what you are doing. Demonstrate though your humble actions how you are making a difference.

<u>Humility in Action</u>

How can you do this, or how could I have done this? Other than simply continuing to do what you are doing, you can contact individual people you work with to tell them about something new you are learning and want to share with them. In other words, don't say, "I'd like to teach you something new;" instead, say, "I'm learning something and want you to join me in learning it." That way, it becomes a shared activity versus an activity where one person dominates the other. The person "learning" with you will be more receptive.

Another way to enlist cooperation—if you have been given the opportunity to learn something new and now need or want to share it with others—is to have the person who taught you, teach others. Even if that means you have to hear a presentation twice or several times, it will give the impression that you are learning it together with everyone else. That does not mean you need to delay implementing your new knowledge where you work until everyone learns it. You can implement your new knowledge and, if asked why you started something before others did, you can simply state that your teacher helped you start while everyone was getting up to speed. In this way, you are still viewed as a student, not a teacher.

Does this seem ridiculous to you, that you need to go to such lengths because others refuse to be taught by you when you learn something new? This strategy is only necessary if the people around you are arrogant. You will have to judge who you work with and decide if they would be amenable to learning from you.
If you judge your coworkers incorrectly and get pushback when trying to teach them, stop, regroup, and try a different approach, as described above.

In some cases, no matter what you do, you might face difficulties. In these cases, try to enlist people who support you to help in the process of teaching.

When all else fails, continue to develop your idea or new program and hope the results will speak for themselves. Show others how it works without reaching out to teach. Sometimes, even this does not work, as was my experience. Sometimes, the only way to proceed is to continue to do your best work, not criticize others for not taking up the new project, and hope that, over time, others will see value in what you do.

The worst thing you can do—which I inadvertently did—is criticize and show the inadequacies of others. Exposing them as stubborn, arrogant, and inflexible only serves to make them mad. Nobody wants to be associated with these characteristics.

Again, lets go back to the example of Mother Teresa. Imagine that instead of continuing to do her work quietly and humbly she started criticizing those around her who were not doing their share to ease suffering. Do you think she would have been seen as the amazing person she was? Most probably not. Would her message have become so widespread and would she have been able to inspire others to continue to do her work around the globe? Most definitely not.

Okay, back to your situation. Let's say you find yourself in the position of trying to teach. You are met with resistance and, in response, you start to criticize others. What do you do now?

You back off, backtrack, and attempt to repair working relationships. You might attempt to find someone else to teach while you continually work behind the scenes, doing your thing. Continue to do what you do best, and, through your quiet work, your results will shine through.

To reiterate, be aware that any damage resulting from your criticism may be irreparable. Cut your losses by stopping the criticism, being humble, and doing your work without enlisting the approval of others. Perhaps this will help heal the chasm you have created and bring others around, or perhaps not. In any case, it is worth a try.

The best approach, however, is to prevent this cycle from starting. Being humble is your goal. Showing humility in what you do is the honey that attracts others, always. Do not be afraid that you will be viewed as ignorant. Arrogance is much too highly rated and certainly much less effective than competence coupled with humility.

CHAPTER 6: R is for RESPECT

"One of the most sincere forms of respect is actually listening to what another has to say." Bryant H. McGill

The definition of respect as per Merriam-Webster is: *To feel admiration for someone or something; to regard someone or something as being worthy of admiration because of good qualities; to act in a way that shows you are aware of someone's rights or wishes.*

Respect includes having an open mind, asking questions, and being open to another's viewpoints, theories, and advice.

Of course, it is very hard to respect someone if that person has not been honest and is arrogant in his or her interactions. In order to not perpetuate antagonism in an individual, we should attempt to be respectful in our interactions with them. That, of course, does NOT mean we act subservient to that person or allow them to step all over us, so to speak, in our discussions. It DOES mean we can respectfully discuss whatever topic needs to be addressed. You can potentially agree to disagree, and, in situations that require buy-in from that person or yourself in order for the team to work cohesively, you can attempt to ensure that the appropriate decisions are made. Appropriate decisions are those that are in the best interest of the whole team, company, office, or whatever your working environment requires.

It is important to note that respect begets respect. This is key to appropriate, effective, and fair interactions. Yes, I know—easier said than done.

Here are some of my personal experiences:

I used to have the following signs hanging in my office: "Don't make me turn on my witch switch," "The witch is in," "Just because I have a vagina doesn't mean I don't have balls. I do, and I will use them as needed."

Why do you think I had to hang up these signs? To me, they were clear statements I needed to make. When someone walked into my office, they had better respect the person in there—namely, me. I went so far as to wear a necklace of testicles of different sizes (a tool used by endocrinologists to evaluate testicular sizes in boys to determine their stage of development). I wore this ornament to remind others—male colleagues, of course—that even though I was a woman, that did not mean I should be shown any less respect for my opinions. The female nurses in my unit loved it and were empowered by my wearing the necklace. Some of my male colleagues chuckled. These were the men that understood what I was going through. Other male colleagues were visibly disturbed by my brazen attitude. I felt I had to do it, though. I was so tired of being treated like a second-class citizen. I felt that wearing this talisman was the only way there would be a visible reminder that I deserved respect, despite being a woman.

Yet, disrespect continued to plague our team. From lies about how much work was done by others, to comments in front of nurses and families about how members of our team practiced as if we lived in the Dark Ages. The degree of disrespect knew no bounds. There was little we could do to counter this. We even tried directly confronting perpetrators of this disrespect. The response was usually, "You misunderstood" or "I was just joking" or my favorite excuse, "That's not true". Talk about a lie to cover up another lie! Remember, two wrongs don't make a right and certainly two lies do not make a truth!

Responding to Disrespect

How do you deal with this level of disrespect—disrespect in front of your team, disrespect in front of your colleagues, disrespect of the team as a whole and, most importantly, disrespect of you as a person?

Let me tell you, it is never easy.
Our team attempted to confront the disrespect head-on by being forthright about what was heard. Despite this, the situation continued. I then went to our supervising physician for our team.

The end result of that meeting was that we were told that all parties needed to talk to each other more often and be respectful of each other. Duh.

This meeting clearly put me at a disadvantage, because I was viewed as the person creating the trouble. Why? I'm not sure. I could say it was a female/male thing, but the supervisor who led the meeting was a woman. She attempted to show she was being "fair". The end result was that nothing happened other than me being placed on the radar screen. I believe she was threatened by my confidence, my truthfulness, and my willingness to NOT tow the party line. In other words, I challenged the status quo. I believe this was the beginning of the countdown to my termination.

In the corporate world, I would venture to say you could find many situations similar to those described above. In a recent study conducted by the Harvard Business Review and Tony Schwartz, written up by Christine Porath, November 19, 2014 in the *Harvard Business Review*, entitled *"Half of employees don't feel respected by their bosses"*. Out of 20,000 employees surveyed, 545 claimed they are not shown respect regularly from their employers.

One example was from a top doctor in a Masters of Medical Management program. He had received harsh criticism and realized he was clueless about how others perceived his mode of communication. He stated he was simply treating residents the way he had been taught.

Perhaps much of what we see in the workplace is people acting the way they see others acting, or people overwhelmed with responsibilities who lash out with disrespectful comments or have rude communication styles. It really does not matter what the reasons are for disrespect in the workplace environment. It makes for an unhealthy and hostile atmosphere, one which makes employees want to quit despite the possible good the company does for them in terms of benefits or salaries.

Another example cited in the research above showed how a company turned around its toxic environment. When the newly appointed CEO of Campbell Soup, Doug Conant, assumed his leadership position, he wrote more than 30,000 individualized notes of thanks to his 20,000 employees. This, in turn, promoted a healthy, positive working environment in which respect was the operative word—so much so that the company went on to exceed the S&P rating five-fold as a result of employees' all-time high performance levels.

What about you, the reader? What scenarios might you find yourself in that are similar to those discussed? I would imagine these would include but not be limited to not being shown respect by your coworkers or boss in their words or actions. Examples as to how this may have played out include situations in which you were not invited to lunch with the rest of the group, weren't cc'd in a memo, didn't receive an email sent to the rest of the group, or were wrongly chastised, which prompted you to address the situation before it got out of hand such as allowing a rumor became reality. Perhaps is was a simple and as devastating as having your ideas be ignored or ridiculed.

Leave Your Emotions at the Door When Confronting Disrespect

In all these situations, I believe it's necessary for you to first confront the offender(s). However, I would advise you to check your anger at the door and not let your emotions get the better of you. Speak firmly but without rancor or anger in your voice.

If this maneuver doesn't work, the next step would be to talk to your supervisor. If the supervisor is part of the problem, go up the chain. Again, starting the conversation with a threat, is not a good approach. Instead, you should attempt to arrange a sit-down to go over issues that are affecting your work environment. During the meeting, explain your side calmly, without emotion, and simply state what is affecting your ability to do your work. Include a description of what your work environment is like. If it is hostile, say so, but back up this claim with examples.

If nothing changes after this meeting and the disrespect continues, you may need to reconsider whether this is truly the right work environment for you. Perhaps you can be transferred, or perhaps you can find another job.

At this point you might ask me, "Why should I be the one to change jobs?" If you do not get the appropriate support from your superiors, you will not win this game. Better to exit on your own accord than continue to struggle daily until finally you are fired, like I was.

Really, it is not a pleasant situation to be in. Trust me on this one.

Where I could have been better and how you can possible improve the situation, is by checking your emotions. I do not mean you should ignore how you feel or repress it. When you are alone or with your significant other, you can fully express your anger. Punch a pillow, scream, do whatever makes you feel better, but do not show this degree of emotion to your coworkers, your team, or your supervisor.

Although I did not realize it at the time, I believe I perpetuated the antagonism within the work environment, which did little to help the situation.

Lesson learned. That's why I am writing this book, so that you will have a better chance of not making the same mistakes I did.

What would I do differently if confronted with the same situation? I might have had a less angry tone and be less outwardly critical. You all know the saying, "It's easier to catch a fly with honey than with vinegar." Take that admonition to heart and learn how to do this, because your job may depend on it.

I'm not sure it would have made a difference in my case; I believe that, for whatever reason, I was a "marked" woman when our group's leadership changed. I never fitted the "corporate mold" they had in mind—adhering to the status quo, so to speak. You might find that this is the case for you, too. At least, if you can identify that you are in a similar situation, you may feel more relieved and less stressed if you do get fired, or you might decide to quit first and not let the absence of corporate policy adversely affect you emotionally. In any case, you will be forewarned and feel more prepared to take on the next challenge.

CHAPTER 7: T is for TEAMWORK

"Unity is strength...when there is teamwork and collaboration, wonderful things can be achieved." Mattie Stepanek

"Alone we can do so little; together we can do so much." Helen Keller

The definition of Teamwork found on BusinessDictionary.com is: *The process of working collaboratively with a group of people in order to achieve a goal.*

In every area of life—personal and work-related—teamwork is a necessity to achieve goals. That's not to say an individual cannot achieve goals without help, but if you think about it, there are no clear examples of this that readily come to mind.

An Olympic contender cannot do it alone. That person needs a coach and family that supports their dream. Researchers cannot discover cures by themselves. They need lab personnel to assist them, grant money to continue their work, and mentors that inspire them to continue. A chef needs the support of the kitchen staff, the growers of produce, the butcher, etc. A student needs the support of family, teachers, etc. to learn and do well. Even a person climbing a mountain needs a sherpa or others to provide support in carrying equipment, supplies, etc. And so it goes with any example you want to use. No one can do it alone, not if they want to achieve the goal they are striving for.

So, teamwork is an integral part of being successful, individually and collectively. Yet, many do not realize this and feel victory must be theirs alone. It's not. It's always about a team and the team effort that got the goal achieved, even if the goal was a personal one, not a team goal.

Here's where I think the problem lies. People believe that because the goal to be achieved is a personal one, achieving it is a personal victory. But, as I illustrated above, it's not. When an individual does not acknowledge this, those who have helped achieve that goal feel slighted and tensions begin, whether it is at work or a home.

To be successful in the corporate world, just as in personal matters, a team is required and the team must be recognized.

Here are some of my personal experiences:

I have to say that, in my particular situation, I had a very intimate team that worked seamlessly together for the goal of providing the best care to our patients brought to our unit for care. Each person knew they were an integral part of our success and, together, we were, indeed, a very happy "family" at work.

The problem arose when colleagues outside our intimate team felt like outsiders. I'm not sure why they felt that way. Although the success of our treatment was not directly linked to them, they were integral to its success because they were the first in line, i.e. the first responders, who identified patients that needed help and arranged for the transport of those patients quickly so we could provide care in a timely manner.

However, they never saw their role as part of the bigger picture or team. They felt isolated even though our team tried to convince them otherwise through outreach education and personal phone calls. They never understood. Instead, they believed that because they needed to transport these patients, they were failures and believed they were looked upon as such. This was never the attitude we conveyed to them, but they felt it, nonetheless.

As our success continued and the community celebrated our achievements, these colleagues became more isolated and less willing to send patients in need of specialized care to us, insisting that these patients were receiving the care they needed. And that was that. The more we tried to explain why what we did was important, the more resistant they were to acknowledge our expertise. As a result, they became further alienated from the ultimate goal.

How do you think I responded? Well, by now you know that I was critical—not at first but toward the end. Initially, I tried to convey information about our therapies that improved long-term outcomes and tried to incorporate everyone as part of the team, but the more obstinate they became, the more critical I became—intensely critical.

How do you think I could have handled it better? Honestly, this question still plagues me to this day. I don't know the answer. I really believed I made a concerted effort to bring everyone into the fold and create a team spirit, not only where I worked specifically but throughout our group of physicians, many of whom were based at other hospitals.

Obviously, however, their perception was not the same as mine.

Examples of Lack of Teamwork in the Corporate World

What examples can we find in the corporate world that resonate with the experiences I had with lack of teamwork? Professional sports teams that display a lack of teamwork may cost themselves a championship. Undesirable business results may stem from a lack of teamwork within a particular business. An example of this might be insurance companies. While one group within the company sells policies, another group within the company may be denying coverage to a client signed by their own agents. How do these two teams work together to promote success within that company? That is the challenge, one that the leader of the company needs to address.

I go back to the example I previously mentioned in the chapter on Achieve, that example being the book, *Start with Why*. Microsoft recently had an overhaul, undergoing a large-scale reorganization. The company wanted its teams to work more cohesively together. This is difficult for any company to do. However, if management considers the premise of "why" they want their company to succeed, they may have a better shot at getting their employees to buy in to the need to work as a team and bring it to fruition.

What You Can do to Encourage Teamwork

What is my advice to you, the reader, for fostering teamwork? Continue your efforts to bring everyone into the team mentality, including those members who may seem more isolated and geographically removed. Have more team meetings and conference calls. When you face pushback, offer compliments on how hard the team is working. Bring them breakfast, lunch, donuts, a cake—whatever you think will make them feel special, and celebrate the small successes. Keep them in the loop about how the project is going. Energize their spirit of teamwork and cooperation. In essence, make them feel special, as special as the team members you work closely with and who are more intimately in the loop, so to speak.

Make sure, above all else, each team member understands why team cooperation is so important. In other words, each member of the team needs to understand "why" they are working so hard. When people understand this, there will be greater buy-in to work together as a team. Without this understanding, you are more likely to have an every-man-for-himself attitude and the cohesive fabric of the organization will disintegrate.

HALT HuRT

To conclude Part 2 of this book, let's review the components of the acronym HALT HuRT: Honesty, Achieve, Learn, Trust, Humility, Respect, and Teamwork. These should serve you well in your quest to survive the corporate world intact and to prevent you being "hurt" within that corporate world, either through criticism or by getting fired.

If you find that no matter what you do, how you proceed, and how completely you invoke the above you continue to be in a bad place, are rejected, put down, or ignored, perhaps it's time to look for a different job. I say this because what you are facing may indicate that your company does not have a corporate soul. There is no internal corporate social responsibility (CSR) policy. Nor is there the culture that it is acceptable to challenge the status quo. If that is the case, no amount of using any of these qualities will help you retain your job, let alone enjoy it. The only exception would be if while using these qualities, the corporation takes notice and, internally, things start to change.

I know that deciding to leave your job is a monumental decision. Certainly, for me, that was the case. Yet, the choice is ever present.

However, you may decide to stay in a less-than-ideal situation—even one that is onerous—if you know what you are dealing with. If you are okay with continuing to do the best job you can despite the difficulties you are facing, by all means, continue.

But be forewarned: You must understand the deficiencies and be willing to accept them. Criticizing the behavior of others will only engender more antagonism and isolate you further. It will create a situation where you are looked upon as a liability rather than an asset. When this starts to happen, your days are numbered, my friend. Be prepared for that, and don't let it catch you by surprise like it did me.

PART 3:

YOU'RE FIRED. NOW WHAT?

CHAPTER 1: The Day After

Perhaps you came upon my book too late to make repairs to the damage done. Perhaps you have already been fired.

In any case, you are still reeling from the shock, am I correct? It's surreal, I know. If you'd been employed for a long time, it seems worse than surreal—it's a nightmare. Even if you were a short-term employee, it still feels like the ultimate punishment. And it is the ultimate punishment. What more could they have done other than arrest you? I would hope that would not be the case, since we are not talking about people who are fired for the right reasons— embezzlement, sexual and or physical harassment, etc.—but for all the wrong reasons, as outlined in the first parts of my book.

So, now what? Well, for starters, take a deep breath. You will go through the grieving process, just as you do when someone close to you dies. In essence, a part of who you are has died. So now you must grieve. It is the important next step toward recovery and moving forward in your life. To not do this would be detrimental to your mental health and probably impede your ability to find another job. So, let's begin.

Grieving

The first step in the grief process is denial or isolation. Allow yourself to start with this emotion or feeling. Within this first step, you will be sad and depressed. Some of you will cry, sob, and maybe even wail. "This can't be happening to me!" That is part of the denial. Your tears, initially, will not be about the sadness of losing your job but rather are generated by denial of the situation. Your tears may creep up on you at the most awkward times in the days ahead. Let them run, but never despair. Do not believe life is over, that there is nothing left. In fact, it's quite the opposite; there is nothing farther from the truth. The world and many possibilities are now open for you to explore. You will be told by many, "When one door closes, another opens." Believe it, because it is true.

Your first responsibility is to stay calm, take deep breaths, and, again, give yourself time to regroup, re-think, and re-invent yourself. So, leverage this stage of grieving by not allowing denial to upstage your ethics and the fortitude you had and continue to have, which allowed you to speak up and make a difference in your last employment. Instead, revisit what you stood for, what you tried to champion and/or whom you tried to protect from bullying, unfair job requirements, unfair pay, or whatever you were trying to do to make your company a better place to work. By doing this, you will defeat this first stage and be closer to healing yourself and finding a better path.

On a more practical side, accept that you have been fired. Don't continue to spend money because you are in this state of denial. Going on a shopping spree will not make it all better nor will it fill the empty void. Again, return to your ethics, which will fill the void and allow you to move on to better things.

Anger…and Revenge

The second step of the grieving process is anger. During this phase, it is likely you will consider the question, "Do I find a lawyer and sue for wrongful termination?" This, of course, is a very important question and one that can be answered only through the thorough examination of your employment contract by an employment lawyer.

Many employment contracts have an "at will" clause that essentially means you can be terminated for no cause. Many contracts will also delineate arbitration as the first step in contesting termination. Arbitration is usually not discoverable through public records. It remains private and usually involves hiring three lawyers—theirs, yours, and an objective party.

Whatever your contract says, discuss it first with your lawyer before contemplating going after them in a fit of revenge. Most of the time, your employer will have much deeper pockets than you have. What I mean by this is that if you lose the case you mount against your former employer, you will more than likely have to pay for all the legal fees involved, theirs and yours, not to mention the emotional and mental toll it will cost you. Any action against your former employers means they will try to find some evidence against you—a disciplinary report, anything. It doesn't matter if this report is five years old or was filed by some crazed employee fired long ago for valid reasons. The company will try to drag your name and reputation through the mud and, believe me, you will not come out clean.

I know that at this point you're thinking, "Wait, that's not fair!" Was it fair that they fired you? Most probably not. The law is not in place to prove innocence; it is in place to show that one party is not guilty. There is a big difference.

So before you take this step, think very clearly. Is the energy you are about to expend worth the possible outcome? Perhaps a better question to ask yourself is, "Can I channel this energy instead to re-invent myself and, in the process, find different opportunities?" If you feel you are opting out of challenging a wrong that was done to you, again, think whether this will change the behavior of that company or your outcome. The answer to both is probably not.

I would venture to say the latter, channeling your energy to re-invent yourself, is more worthwhile for your sanity and your future success in life, because, at the end of the day, even if you win your case, what would your former employer offer you? Your old job back? Would it be worthwhile taking it back? Don't you think they will make your life even more miserable than before?

If you think you might have a chance for a settlement, again, be very careful and consider what we have just discussed. Corporations do not like to lose. They also have deeper pockets and more high-powered lawyers than you could hope to hire, and, in the end, would probably win the final decision.

When you're faced with termination, the first and only question you might be asked by your employer as you finalize your paperwork is, "Do you want to resign rather than be fired?"

First of all, there is no shame in stating to others, even other possible future employers, that you were fired. This is true, of course, if the cause of being fired is not your fault! That is the premise of this whole book. We are not discussing those folks that should have been fired but rather those who were wrongfully terminated!

Do not be ashamed. You will have the ability to explain your circumstances every chance you get. In fact, if you choose to resign, which still probably means you need to leave your place of employment immediately, others will know the decision to resign was not yours. So, what's the difference? You might as well get fired so you can explain your circumstance to others and get some financial compensation.

What I mean by financial compensation includes the following. In some contracts, by resigning and needing to leave immediately, you most likely will NOT get severance pay. That is because, if you resign truly of your own accord, you will usually give your employer 90 days to find a replacement. When you are asked to resign, you leave immediately. If you allow yourself to get fired, you will most likely get some amount of severance pay.

Another point to consider is that when you resign, you will be unable to collect unemployment insurance, which we will talk about later on. This may be critical to consider, since you might be without employment for a while and will need all the financial help available to get you through until you find your next job.

Therefore, use your anger not to develop a plan of revenge but as a platform to propel you toward a brighter future. Use the anger to energize you to begin to strategize what you need to do next, how you will develop yourself.

Do not let the anger consume you and blind you to the potentials that lie ahead. Let it wash over you, let it dissipate and make room to continue the grieving process with this next step.

<u>Bargaining</u>

The third stage of the grieving process is bargaining. You will try to bargain, in your own mind, what you need to do to get your old job back. You will bargain with God or the Universe to help you find gainful employment. You will bargain with your own self about how to become a better person, how to apologize to the old guard. You will try to apologize about your job loss to others, stating that maybe if you had done better, stayed quiet, not challenged others, etc., etc., etc., ad infinitum! Enough! Leave "mea culpa" to the sinners. You are not one of them!

You were fired. This turn of events was caused not because you were at fault but because you cared about what was happening at your job, to others, to the company, or to society as a whole. It doesn't matter anymore. You no longer have to make excuses; you now can speak the truth. Be proud of the fact you can look at yourself in the mirror and respect the image looking back. That is worth more than your salary ever was. I would venture to say that those you have left behind cannot look at themselves in the mirror with any respect. Perhaps they don't care, but that is not your problem. Move on.

So how can you make this stage—bargaining—another step toward healing your grief?

Well, the definition of bargaining is essentially to compromise. However, the last thing you want to do is compromise who you are and what you stand for. Therefore, use bargaining as the antithesis of what happened to you. Demonstrate to yourself and others that, indeed, bargaining was never part of what you wanted to do to maintain your job. It is a worthless exercise in trying to accomplish any goal. If, in your previous job, you had resorted to bargaining, you would have lost part of the respect you garnered for yourself and from others in the stand you actually took, whatever it was.

Therefore, understand that by not bargaining, you became stronger. Using bargaining now to heal the pain would only set you back. Recognize that bargaining is just another essential step in grieving, a natural progression of your thoughts as you process what you have gone through. Again, let it pass and continue to move onward into the next stage so you can eventually complete the grieving process and start taking positive steps toward a new future.

Depression

Depression is not your friend, but it is the necessary next and fourth step toward healing. What is its purpose and how can you turn it around to help you move forward? These are two vital questions.

Perhaps depression is a way for your brain to reboot your emotional state of mind and prevent it from acting impulsively. What do I mean by this? Imagine that you are now in the throes of depression and decide that you might as well give up looking for work; you believe you will never find another job. Or, worse yet, you decide that you aren't worthy of working in the capacity you were before and, therefore, you start looking for a menial job. That is not to say that jobs that only pay the minimum rate should be shunned, but, by accepting less than what you deserve based on your experience and education, you may lose the opportunity of a lifetime or, at the very least, a position that is actually matched to your talents and education.

You must keep looking for work and wait to find a job suitable to your education and experience. How do you get out of your funk while you continue to search? This is important because going to an interview in a state of depression will not serve you well. It is similar to going to an interview angry about your previous experience. Neither emotional state will allow the prospective employer to see the true gem you are, the talents you can bring, and the experiences you have had, including your experience of getting fired and the reasons why that happened.

I believe that to emerge from a depressed state, you must begin to believe in yourself again. Look in the mirror at the person looking back. Remember why you respect the image looking back. Remember the sacrifices you made to get the education and experience you obtained. It was not handed to you on a silver platter. Most likely, you had to work hard to get where you are today. Once you recognize these facts and recognize that you will be an invaluable asset to whoever hires you, then and only then will you be able to shake that depression off. Then and only then will you be able to stand proudly before another person during an interview and let them know why they need to hire you right then and there.

Now you can move on to the last step of this massive grieving process, acceptance.

Acceptance

Acceptance means you finally can say to yourself, "I was fired" without feeling the wind being knocked out of you, without tearing up, and without feeling the pity you have been carrying on your back. "Okay, I got fired. Okay, this is the reason I got fired. Okay, I can still look at myself in the mirror and like what I see looking back. Okay, karma is a real bitch and I hope I see it played out." Right? You have finally accepted what happened, you are finally not sorry for yourself, you finally can move on with your life and find another job equally if not more fulfilling.

Run with this, get excited again, take on the world and show it what you have to offer. Be creative, be spontaneous, dare to find a new path and a new purpose. Remember the quote from Carly Fiorina, the ex-CEO of Hewlett-Packard, that I mentioned earlier: "I challenged the status quo, so I was fired." Bravo! I can relate to that and I believe most of you reading this book can too.

Once you embark on this new journey and set your sights on the horizon ahead, it will suddenly be over—the grief, that is. The veil will lift, the clouds will part, and you will see clearly what lies ahead and what is required of you to succeed in your endeavors.

So, "the day after," which really describes the "days after" and involves the initial shock followed by this grieving period, is over. You survived. In fact, you survived a better person for it. That is not to say the wound is healed. It is still fresh, fresh enough that even after the grieving is over, you will still tear up when you talk about your experience to a friend. However, the pain is less, the intensity is gone, and what has replaced those feelings is a melancholy that probably will always be there. Why? Because more than likely the job you lost was more intimately involved with the person you are—your identity—than you realized.

To prove this, ask yourself how you introduced yourself to others, after you said your name. Were you just John or Jane Doe, or were you "Hi, I'm John/Jane, the teacher at this school, the manager at this store, the engineer, the doctor, the lawyer?" Of course, that was who you were and will always be, even if your career takes a different turn.

Don't you think I will always be "Cristina, the subspecialist, the Medical Director?" Yes, of course, even though I am now an author and an assistant clinical professor. I will always think of myself as a healer. That will never change. Why? What if your career takes a turn that is opposite to what you did before? It really doesn't matter, because who you were will always be a part of who you are and who you will continue to be until you exit this life. It has made you the person that is reading this book.

I can only liken the truth of this to the analogy used about wrinkles: Each line tells a story and is part of the fabric of who you are as a person. Your job history is the same thing, only it is internal, not cosmetic or superficial. Your identity, through the descriptive lens of your career, is part of your personality, your hopes and dreams, and your very being. As you embark on a new career, it will never replace the work you did in the past. It will incorporate those experiences and your previous ways of thinking to make your future experiences that much more individualized than the next person with a similar career. The way you think, how you respond to others, and how you conduct yourself at your new job incorporates all your past experiences and gives you greater satisfaction and a sense of richness in these new experiences you never thought possible.

And so, the period called "the day after" ends and you are faced with the next phase of your new life, a phase I like to call a "Time to Reflect." The immediacy of being fired is over. You have survived the grieving process and have come out the other side, clearer in your vision as to who you are as a person and what your beliefs are. Through it all, your identity has stayed intact. Congratulations!

CHAPTER 2: A Time to Reflect

Well, the "days after" have come and gone, as has your process of grieving. You've grieved. Now what?

What a minute. Didn't we talk about the time to reflect in the last chapter? Not really. You first had to process the steps of grieving and see where that took you. Now you are ready for the real work. The grieving process was just the preparation piece; preparation for your psyche and preparation for your first steps toward a new, re-invented you.

"Wait," you say, "I don't want to re-invent myself. I want to stay the same, find a similar job, change as little as possible in my life, keep the status quo."

Well, first of all, it may be very difficult for you to be able to do this because you are a different person than you were prior to getting fired. Something shifted in your being during your healing process and will never be the same. The shift may be small, it may be almost indiscernible, but it's there.

You are a different person. You see the world differently. Perhaps with less than rose-colored glasses, perhaps with more caution about other's sincerity, and certainly with some self-doubt of your own worth in society. It will not be easy to initially say those words: "I was fired." With time, this will change. The implication and stigma still remain that, obviously, you must have done something wrong to suffer this punishment. However, you have just gone through this grief, this healing process, and have come out the other end knowing your getting fired had nothing to do with any derelict performance on your part. Yet, it is still difficult to muster those words. It bears repeating—it will get easier, I assure you. As you continue to tell your story to others, you will accelerate your ability to reflect on your next steps.

So what are those steps? Let's list them.

Reflection #1: Ask yourself this question: What do I want to do and accomplish from this point forward? What are my dreams and aspirations?

These are important questions to reflect on, because your previous job/career may have been acquired secondary to another's wishes. Perhaps your parents thought it would be in your best interest to follow medicine or perhaps your best friend decided to go into business and you thought, "Why not? I'm good with numbers and I might as well make a good living." No matter who influenced you before, break out of the mold and see yourself in a different light.

"Wait a minute," you say. "No one influenced me. I chose that career path of my own accord. Now what?" Well, perhaps you did. Perhaps no one helped you in your decision making. Perhaps your previous job was your passion all along. You have two choices at this point: try to return to your previous career or re-invent yourself—discover a new passion and run with it. What you decide will depend on many factors, including whether you are responsible financially and emotionally for others or answer to yourself alone. Are there opportunities to resume your previous career where you presently live, or must you move? If you have to move, is that feasible, if others have to be taken into account?

Whatever your answers are—and there are no right or wrong answers—make sure you are genuinely happy with your responses. Remember, the status quo is always easier but never better. Don't accept the status quo just because it is easier; only accept it if it feels right.

You may have to leave your comfort zone to answer these questions, but you will be happier for it when you ask yourself what makes you happy rather than what makes others happy or accepting the status quo just because it seems easier than making a change.

Once you reflect on all of this—which, by the way, may take a while—and come up with answers that make you happy (perhaps a little scared, but happy and excited nonetheless), it's time for the next reflective question to assist you in your journey.

Reflection #2: Okay, you've done some hard work and you've decided what you want out of life from this point forward. It doesn't matter if you choose to return to your previous career or to forge ahead to new horizons. It only matters how you re-enter the working world and how you re-establish your career path, whether it's a familiar or new one. This reflection has to do with "How do I proceed?" after you answer "What path do I choose?"

If you are re-entering the same career, you will need to face job prospects in a state of calmness, self-assurance, and self-confidence to be able to explain why you no long are working where you worked before. At this point, there cannot be any room for self-doubt, regrets, or even the smallest inkling of a vengeful attitude. Any of these projections to your future employer will only serve to alienate you as someone who is not ready to move on. A future employer knows that self-pity only reaps poor work ethics and the desire for revenge only indicates you will be an angry employee, unwilling to work with others. There is no room for these manifestations of unfinished business on your part in your next career.

If your decision is moving to another career choice, it is likely you explored other passions at some point in your life. Perhaps, like me, you realize you love to write. Perhaps another creative outlet such as painting, sculpting, dancing, or acting is what you love. Perhaps you realize you may need further education to pursue your next career. I've seen doctors become lawyers, lawyers become doctors, and teachers become actors. I think you get the idea of what I am talking about. It is a little like graduating college with one degree and pursuing another career unrelated to the degree you've obtained. That's okay. You need to be comfortable in your own skin. Always remember it is your life, not anyone else's, and only you can make it a happy one.

Wherever this reflection takes you, be assured you are a step closer to achieving your dream job, whether it's within the same career path or a different one. Also remember: If you are returning to your previous career, be wary of the employer you choose to work with. Make sure their ethics are your ethics. Otherwise, you may find yourself in the same predicament as before.

Reflection #3: Okay, you've answered "What do I want to do?" and "How do I proceed to do what I want to do?" The next important reflection is: "How can I be successful doing what I want to do?" Well, the good news is, you are partly on your way. Success is not measured in promotions or titles or salary. It's measured in the satisfaction you derive from your new job, whether it's within your same career or a different one. Success means you are achieving new goals. You are ready and willing to continue to pursue your passion.

Embrace this time. Even if you are in a job within your same career, you will be meeting new people, new avenues will open up to you, and new paths within this well-traveled career will appear and offer you insight you never had before. This is even more evident if this career is a totally new path in a completely different direction than the one you knew before. Not only will you be meeting new people but the ideas you will be presented with and the working models and experiences will most definitely open entirely new vistas, which, in turn, will open subsets of other vistas still unknown to you. I know this sounds vague, but when you start experiencing this, you will better understand what I am trying to describe.

So, to summarize this reflection, your ability to feel successful will occur gradually and, at first, internally. You will feel happy and energized every morning, eager to face new challenges. Secondarily, your success will manifest externally as those around you start acknowledging your accomplishments and respect your vision within that career choice.

There is no doubt that hard work on your part will be necessary, not only to prove to yourself your own self-worth but also to demonstrate to those around you that you have not only survived being fired, you've used it to discover a more authentic self. You are committed to succeeding in your endeavors with integrity, ethics, and grace. When you can demonstrate this to yourself and others, you've made it. You have succeeded and surpassed your goal of surviving another day and instead are living your dream, doing what makes you happy, and hopefully helping the world become a better place because of it.

CHAPTER 3: Moving Forward

Well, you've made it! You have survived the day(s) after, you have reflected on what your next career moves are, and you are ready to move forward.

You may have gotten some ideas about your next step in the last chapter as you were reflecting, so you may be already moving forward. However, there are some nitty-gritty details we should examine of which you should be aware and implementing.

Unemployment Benefits

The first consideration, of course, is monetary. You have been fired. Under federal and state laws, you are entitled to unemployment benefits within your state. Unemployment insurance is financed through federal and state payroll taxes. In order to receive benefits, you must have worked for at least one quarter during the previous year. So, please contact your state government to see if you are eligible. Google "unemployment benefits" for your state and you should be directed to the link that explains eligibility and provides access to an online application. If you quit or werc fired for cause, you might not be eligible. If you are laid off or fired without cause, you should be able to file. However, again, you will need to apply within your own state for eligibility and it may take a few weeks before you start to receive payments.

The amount you receive will be determined by your previous salary, how long you have worked, and whether you are actively looking for another job. Although the payment will be a fraction of your previous salary (and dependent on the state in which you worked), you should apply for it. You've paid into this fund as an employee, so you are entitled to file, and it may help you survive until you find another job. A note of caution: You should file either as soon as you are fired or as soon as your severance package, if there was any, has been expended. If you delay filing, you may be disqualified.

Deciding on a Career Path

Once you have done this, what are your next steps? If you have had time to reflect, you should be taking the next steps toward creating a new career path, either by looking for another job in your same area of expertise or starting the process of re-inventing yourself in your new career path.

In my case, I was fired from a highly specialized medical profession and my contract had a non-compete clause that prevented me from working in the same field where I lived, i.e., I would have had to move out of state to pursue my specialty. Therefore, I had to re-invent my professional self. As a physician, I knew I could teach, so I started looking at community colleges, local universities, and our local medical school to teach basic sciences.

I had also started to write prior to being fired (this is my second book), so I continued to hone in on my writing career.

I have also looked at life coaching, because I have been told I have inspired young students in the past and I love the feeling of helping others live a better life.

You must discover what your passions are, which I hope you have accomplished in your "time to reflect" period after the shock of being fired has dissipated.

What if, after much reflection, you do not want to re-invent yourself? What if you want to stay within your same profession but there is nothing available to you where you presently live? Well, you will have to make some changes, either physically or, if that is not possible, pick a second-choice career. You might find you are just as happy, or other opportunities might present themselves to you unexpectedly because of this slight shift in your career path.

Job Seeking

Whatever path you choose, you are now ready to walk out the door and create a new life for yourself. Unless you decide to become self-employed or start a work-from-home job, you will need to fill our applications, send resumes, and go for interviews.

Make sure your resume or Curriculum Vitae is up to date. Although this seems like obvious advice, you might be surprised how outdated it is if you've been working for a long time. Especially remember to correct your previous employment as terminated rather than current.

At interviews, when asked, be honest about what happened at your previous job. Do not lie about being fired, or why you were fired. Any employer worth their salt will find your honesty refreshing.

You also may find you might need to take some refresher courses or get an alternate degree to pursue your next profession. As an example, when I was contemplating becoming a life coach, I realized this would require some further training.

Again, during this period, I cannot emphasize to you, the reader, how important collecting those unemployment benefits might be. They may be the cushion you need to get through the next steps and take away some of the monetary stress of losing your salary.

How to Make Sure the Past Doesn't Repeat Itself

Once you have landed your next dream job or embarked on a new career path, how can you prevent what previously happened to you from happening again? First, prior to committing to your next job, make sure you feel comfortable with your new employer's work ethics. Prior to signing on, use social media to investigate the company's or person's history, reviews, and any grievances filed against them. Ask if the company has an internal corporate social responsibility (CSR) policy. If you find red flags, perhaps you need to continue to look elsewhere. You do not want to be placed in a similar position as before, which might put you at risk for being fired.

If you have concerns but are unsure of the validity of what you found in your research, be direct during an interview. Ask questions and go with your gut. Believe it or not, there are nerve endings in our gastrointestinal tracts that connect to our brain and help us with critical thinking. Trust your instincts. If it doesn't feel right, no matter how good the salary and/or benefits are, don't take the job unless you are desperate financially. In those situations, be cautious. Half the battle is knowing what you are walking into. Leave the position as soon as you can, as soon as another possibility comes your way. Continue to work within your ethics. If those ethics are compromised, you will have to make a decision as to what you need to do, what you can do, and whether you are more at risk staying than leaving. Those are questions only you can answer.

Once you decide which job is the right fit for you, how do you prevent what happened to you before? Go back and reread the first and second parts of this book. Familiarize yourself with corporate social responsibility—specifically, internal policies as well as the qualities necessary to survive and thrive in the corporate world.

Never forget HALT HuRT. This, of course, is not a guarantee that you will never face challenges again. You will, but hopefully, you will have better tools to deal with them. Half the battle is finding the right group of people to work with; the other half is knowing how to behave within any group so that you will survive and ultimately succeed.

When you have accomplished this, you can help your organization continue to grow and, in turn, it will help you further grow and succeed, ultimately teaching the newcomers how to behave so that everyone wins.

Your and your company's success will be the supreme revenge on your previous employer. I can assure you, they won't ultimately succeed. It might take some time, but eventually a company not dedicated to working with ethics and integrity, not having a soul, and always using the bottom line as its gauge of success will ultimately fail.

EPILOGUE

I initially wrote this book to support those in the workforce who are worried about getting fired or have already been fired. As a member of the latter group, I felt the need to explore what I learned through this process and share my knowledge with others. Writing this book has been very cathartic; however, in the end, it became more than that. It became a how-to guide, created to help others who are going through similar situations.

To further validate the reason I wrote this book, a recent Gallop poll indicated that over 60% of the workforce is fearful of getting fired. Therefore, I thought this book might help all of you who have worried about losing your job or are otherwise disenfranchised in your present work environment and are wondering how to change this.

Some of the issues employees presently face are secondary to the world changing exponentially, both in the workplace as well as in the personal realm.

Our ability to communicate through social media, connect to 24/7 news channels, and negotiate across the oceans as we did across the sales counter in years gone by have made our world truly a village. What affects someone on the other side of the globe affects each of us, daily, as if they were living next door.

Why is this so important in the context of job searches, career development, staying employed, and feeling good about your job/career? Because this world, this village we call home, operates more in unison than as separate nations when it comes to information shared and goals achieved. Most important are the consequences of actions taken to benefit the bottom line over the greater good.

What I believe to be true is that our success, as individuals, is measured not in dollars but in improving our world and making it a better place to live. This involves demanding of ourselves and others that we keep this important concept in mind. In other words, our work should be based on ethics and integrity. Without these, a job is just a job and the bottom line will always trump the greater good. We discussed this in Part 1, but it needs to be emphasized because all the qualities we discussed in Part 2 eventually boil down to promoting ethics and integrity over all else.

This means understanding that what is asked of you as an employee or as an employer will determine whether you, as an individual, are suited for a job and also determines the longevity of any major corporation. Its longevity will, in turn, be determined by its buy-in to ethics and integrity as its core value system. Therefore, first and foremost, you must be able to clearly understand what your role is within a company, what is expected of you in that role, and how that role fits with your inherent value as a person.

Ethics and integrity. Let's review one more time what these two words mean.

Ethics: Because we are talking about jobs and businesses, let me relay to you the definition of this word in the BusinessDictionary.com: *Ethics is the basic concepts and fundamental* principles *of decent human behavior. It includes study of universal values such as the essential equality of all men and women, human and natural rights, obedience to the law of the land, and concern for health, safety, and the natural environment.* Essentially, ethics describes what is considered moral behavior, right or wrong.

Integrity: In Merriam-Webster's definition, integrity is *the quality of being honest and fair.*
As per Wiktionary, the definition of integrity is *a steadfast adherence to a strict moral or ethical code.*

So, in essence, integrity is the vehicle that carries the ethical code.

Both are related to each other and one cannot exist without the other. The qualities described in Part 2 of this book can only operate within the realm of ethics and integrity. This is the foundation of what corporate social responsibility is built on. Lack of these traits will not allow internal and external CSR policies to grow and thrive.

If who you work for is out of sync with these two, essential moral standards and has no CSR to ensure that a corporate "soul" exists, you will be in danger of forfeiting who you are as a person and what you stand for. Could you find work in a company or corporation that does not honor ethics and integrity? Yes, you could, but all the qualities we have discussed are irrelevant to your success within that type of company.

Our discussion of the qualities necessary to survive and thrive in the corporate world was based on the clear assumption that we were describing jobs or careers within

ॐ

companies or corporations that valued ethics and integrity and therefore adhere to CSR policies. All of these are essential to succeed within a corporation as well as essential for that corporation to survive and thrive within the boundaries of ethics and integrity.

There is no place for the opposites of these qualities to exist—not for the individual and not for a company. Dishonesty, complacency, stagnation, distrust, arrogance, disrespect, and lack of teamwork all work against a person's or company's ability to survive in today's working world and will result in a lack of ethics and integrity. Hypocrisy is, in fact, the opposite of integrity. Failure as an individual and as a company to be successful in today's world, is the direct result of the opposites of those qualities we have discussed, being adhered to. I am reiterating this to bring home the importance of these qualities. Without them, our world will eventually fall into chaos and disrepair, a situation of every man for himself. With this attitude, progress would come to a complete halt.

When looking at the process necessary for re-entry into the workforce after you have been fired, it is important to take to heart the recommendations set forth in this book. You must be able to do the work of recovery, including grieving, so you can emerge ready to rejoin the workforce and contribute your talents for the betterment of our world.

In the Appendices are worksheets to help you nurture these qualities in yourself as well as to help you navigate the grief process and re-entry into the workforce.

I hope that this book has helped you identify what is truly important to survive and thrive in your current job. If you found this book after you were fired, I hope it helps you through the process of finding another job or career. Once found, I also hope it further assists you in being successful in your new endeavors by understanding the qualities necessary to survive, thrive, and feel good about what you do.

Together—one person at a time, one job at a time, one corporation at a time—we can accelerate progress in making our lives more enjoyable and profitable, and contribute to the betterment of humanity.

APPENDIX #1

WORKSHEETS FOR EACH QUALITY

Below you will find worksheets to assist you to nurture each quality discussed in the book as well as worksheets to assist you, if you have already been fired, to get back on your feet, so to speak.

There are no wrong or right answers. My intention is to get you to think carefully about how you answer each question and use those answers to assist you to become successful and fulfilled in your profession—in other words, the best that you can be.

Life is too short not to be happy in what you do and how you live each day.

WORKSHEETS FOR PART 1

WORKSHEET #1: HONESTY

1. In what part of your present or past job has honesty been lacking?

- Is it or was it in interpersonal relationships?

- In hours worked?

- In results obtained?

- In your or others' abilities to take care of a problem?

2. Why do you think honesty is or wasn't valued?

3. How can you bring honesty to the forefront in your present job?

4. How can you make sure honesty is valued, nurtured, and mandated in your future job?

NOTES for WORKSHEET #1: HONESTY

WORKSHEET #2: ACHIEVE

Do you find there is a lack of desire to achieve by others or yourself in your current job?

Was a lack of desire to achieve the reason you lost your job?

In your current or future job, how will you promote the need to achieve within yourself and/or in others?

How would you describe what achievement is to you personally?

Why do you believe the need to achieve is important to insure success in either your present job or in any future job?

Once you have achieved your goal, are there other goals you can identify to work toward?

NOTES for WORKSHEET #2: ACHEIVE

WORKSHEET #3: LEARN

Why is the need to continuously learn important to you in your current job?

In any future job, why will it be important to understand you always need to learn something new from others?

How can you promote to others the importance of learning new things without sounding arrogant?

How can you teach new things to others without sounding arrogant?

If learning is not a valued quality where you presently work, do you believe you can continue to grow as a professional?

Does being challenged with new learning tasks make you feel inadequate or stupid?

NOTES for WORKSHEET #3: LEARN

NOTES for WORKSHEET #3: LEARN

WORKSHEET #4: TRUST

Do you trust the people you work with and/or for?

Do the people you work with or for trust you?

If trust is not evident within your work environment, how does this adversely affect your work?

How can you help build trust in your workplace?

How will you know you can trust others or that you are trusted in a future job?

Is there any evidence that dishonesty is at play where you currently work or in a new job you are considering?

Is the dishonesty you see or experience superficial, or is it of concern for ethical reasons?

NOTES for WORKSHEET #4: TRUST

WORKSHEET #5: HUMILITY

Do you come across as humble or arrogant?

Do you think showing humility at work implies you are a pushover?

How can you show humility without being seen as weak?

In your mind, does humility equate with lack of knowledge?

How can being humble improve your image at work?

How can you help others acquire humility?

Can you be humble and still be a leader?

NOTES for WORKSHEET #5: HUMILITY

WORKSHEET #6: RESPECT

What are aspects of your current or past job that demonstrate the quality of respect?

Why is being respectful of others important to promote a cohesive working environment?

Do you believe that constructive criticism goes against being respectful?

How can you tell if others are disrespectful to you?

In what ways do those you respect improve your work environment?

Do you feel you are respectful enough, or do you need to up the ante?

If you are accused of being disrespectful at work, how can you change or demonstrate that you are not?

NOTES for WORKSHEET # 6: RESPECT

WORKSHEET # 7: TEAMWORK

Do you feel you can work better and accomplish more if others leave you alone?

Do you believe teamwork is overrated and decreases work efficiency?

If others say you are not a team player, how can you change that perception?

Do you respect others as part of your team, or are you using other people to promote yourself?

If a project succeeds, do you take all the credit for it or do you include everyone who made the success possible?

How can you ensure that teamwork is valued where you work or in your next job?

If there is more than one team at work, how can you promote cohesiveness among the teams?

Does competition eliminate the value of teamwork?

NOTES for WORKSHEET #7: TEAMWORK

APPENDIX #2

WORKSHEETS FOR PART 2

WORKSHEET #1: The Day(s) After

The following are the stages of grieving. How can you use each one to heal and help you move on?

Denial/Isolation

Anger

Bargaining

Depression

Acceptance

After you have gone through each step of the grieving process, what emotions do you then feel? Are you hopeful and excited about a new start, or are do you feel tentative and scared to move on in your life?

Do you need to seek professional help, career counseling, or a support group?

NOTES on WORKSHEET #1: THE DAY(S) AFTER

WORKSHEET #2: Time to Reflect

Questions to consider:

- Can you stay within your same profession?

- Do you need to seek a new profession?

- Are there any other work passions that excite you?

- Do you need to get a different or additional education for a new career path?

- What will be the time and cost to do so?

- Are you willing to move to stay in the same profession?

- You are being given a new opportunity to start fresh—how will you use it?

- If new opportunities present themselves to you, are you willing to look at what those opportunities are, even if they diverge from your present profession or career path?

- Are you willing to start from the bottom and work your way to the top of your new-found profession?

- How much are you willing to sacrifice—monetarily, emotionally or otherwise—to acquire a new profession?

NOTES for WORKSHEET #2: TIME TO REFLECT

WORKSHEET #3: Moving Forward

Review your previous contract with a lawyer.

Within that contract, specifically look at the grievance clause, severance compensation, non-compete agreement, and whether your termination was "at will" or could it be argued as wrongful.

After you determine what your contract says and allows you to do, decide whether you can sue, arbitrate, or take the severance package that comes with getting fired. These decisions are very important. Choose wisely, using your brain and your lawyer's advice, not your emotions.

Apply for unemployment insurance if you are eligible. You will need to find out what eligibility means for the state in which you last worked.

Start the education process if you need to for any new career path you wish to pursue. You will need credentials to prove you are eligible for any job you interview for within that new profession.

Once you have gone through the above processes, it's time to look for new employment.

- Check that your Curriculum Vitae or resume is up to date.

- Apply for jobs that meet your ethical as well as your professional criteria.

- Be forthright during the interview process.

- Do not lie on your application or during your interview

- Explain to the person interviewing you what you are looking for and the qualities of the prospective job that are important to you. You may think that stating these qualities might make you sound arrogant, but it won't. On the contrary, you will be viewed as a competitive applicant who knows what he or she wants and believes that these qualities are important for success, both individually and for the company.

- Once you acquire a new job, do not forget about these qualities. Keep the acronym HALT HuRT ever present and teach others.

Finally, good luck in your new job. I wish you much success in your career and hope your life is better for it. I hope that this book assisted you in finding your way back.

If you have found that this book was helpful to you, please share it with others going through similar situations.

I have written an accompanying adult humor book on getting fired that parallels the qualities needed to be successful, as described in this book. The title of this book is "Shut the F*ck Up or Else You'll Get Fired!" I think you will find it a fun read and a good way to relieve the tension involved with getting fired. Remember, *"laughter is the best medicine!"*

I would also love to hear your stories of how this book helped you through your journey. Please visit my website if you would like to share your stories with me, ask questions or leave comments. www.mpwrwmn.com. Thank you.

About the Author

Cristina Carballo-Perelman, M.D., has been a specialized physician for over twenty-seven years.

Although she stayed true to her ethics and her professional dedication, she was fired. In this book, the author takes the reader along on her personal journey through the trauma of being fired— the reasons why, the steps to recovery, and her transformation into a new career.

She explores with the reader the grieving process necessary to survive. She also gives the reader advise on the qualities needed to succeed in today's work environment without losing one's soul.

Fired: Challenging the Status Quo and the Aftermath is essential reading, not only for employees who want to do what is best without fear of being terminated but also to help employers bring grace, understanding, and compassion to their companies by adopting corporate social responsibility policies that allow their employees and their businesses to thrive.

The author lives in Scottsdale, Arizona, with her husband and her two dogs and one cat. Her daughter, who just finished her B.S. in Biology, is presently pursuing a career in healthcare.